GRACE IN ECLIPSE
A Study on Eternal Rewards

GRACE IN ECLIPSE
A Study on Eternal Rewards

by
Zane C. Hodges
Professor of New Testament
Dallas Seminary

REDENCIÓN VIVA

Box 141167
Dallas, Texas 75214

Cover photograph by
David Edmonson

© 1985 by

REDENCIÓN VIVA

ISBN 0-9607576-3-5

Printed in the United States of America.

TABLE OF CONTENTS

FOREWORD

A need has arisen in the evangelical community for a return to the simple message of salvation by faith alone. Salvation and discipleship have been confused by pastors and evangelists in the current trend to front-load the gospel message. In *Grace in Eclipse* Prof. Zane Hodges makes an important contribution to the movement that seeks to reestablish a biblical gospel message.

In this timely work, Prof. Hodges presents an exegetically oriented treatise on the doctrine of rewards and their relationship to the gospel. Through a careful analysis of the pertinent passages of Scripture, he argues conclusively that the believer's faithfulness or unfaithfulness to the cause of Christ in this life will result in both rewards and regrets in the life hereafter. In refocusing our attention on the eternal consequences of obedience or disobedience to God, Prof. Hodges has surfaced for us the biblical perspective on sin in the life of the believer.

It is my prayer that this book will be read by pastors and evangelists everywhere and will thus be used by God to put an end to what Prof. Hodges has rightly described as an "eclipse of grace."

Charles F. Stanley
Pastor, First Baptist Church of Atlanta, Ga.

PROLOGUE

Jim has been a Christian for only a short time. Last night, in a group Bible study, he was introduced to the subject of eternal rewards. This morning he is excited by the thought of running a victorious race for God.

On his break at work, Jim shares some of his new-found insights with a fellow Christian named Frank.

"Rewards, huh?" says Frank. "Isn't that just a little selfish?"

"What do you mean?" replies Jim. It hadn't sounded selfish last night.

"Well, what I mean is this," Frank begins, with a slight tone of condescension. "We really ought to serve God because we love Him and are grateful for what He's done for us. We don't need rewards to motivate our Christian life."

"Oh!" says Jim. He can feel the air going out of his balloon.

"Besides," Frank continues, "you don't really think some Christians are going to be a lot better off in heaven than other Christians, do you?"

"Well, I hadn't quite thought about it that way," Jim admits with a trace of dejection in his voice.

"Look, Jim," Frank pursues his theme, "good works are what every Christian does just as a natural result of believing in Christ. That's part of what it means to be a Christian in the first place."

"But we're not *saved* by works," Jim objects.

"No, of course not! But the Bible says a tree is known by its fruit, so if you're really saved, the Christian life will be as natural as fruit-bearing."

"What does that have to do with it?" Jim wants to know.

"It's simple, Jim." Frank moves in for the kill. "If Christian living is part of being a Christian, why should God reward us for it?"

"You mean there are no rewards *at all*?"

"No, I don't mean that exactly," Frank responds. "But all Christians are overcomers and all of them will wear crowns some day. This stuff about Christians failing and being defeated is a bunch of nonsense!"

"Don't we all fail sometimes, Frank?" Jim is a bit put off by the whole discussion.

"Of course we do!" Frank's tone is edged with exasperation. "But good works are our Christian duty, and if you're not doing them at all you ought to examine whether you were ever saved to begin with."

"So you're telling me there are no real losers in the Christian race, is that it?" Jim is very skeptical about *that* idea.

"That's right, Jim!" Frank is emphatic. "The only reason people talk about rewards a lot is because they really don't understand what the Christian life is all about. — Hey! Wasn't that the whistle to get back to work?"

"Yes, I guess break time is over," Jim agrees.

Actually, Jim was glad to get back to work. There had been something depressing about that whole conversation. It was just as if some kind of shadow had been cast across a path that a few moments before had seemed so bright and thrilling.

A shadow *had* crossed his path! In fact that shadow was very much a part of the evangelical scene within which Jim now moved. Its darkening effects were in evidence everywhere.

To put it plainly, grace was in eclipse.

CHAPTER

1

GRACE IN ECLIPSE

"But I discipline my body and bring it into subjection, lest, when I have preached to others, I myself should become disqualified" (1 Cor. 9:27).

With these words, the Apostle Paul expresses a thought that is shocking to many modern Christians. Taken at face value, his words reveal that he seriously entertained the possibility of ending his Christian life as a failure. In fact this failure, says Paul, could come after years of preaching. So to avoid it, he dealt very strictly with his own body and its impulses to do evil.

Many have thought that Paul's reference to disqualification meant that he was in danger of losing his salvation. This idea was encouraged by the familiar King James translation, "lest . . . I myself should be a castaway." But Paul firmly believed that God would ultimately bring those He called and justified to glory (Rom. 8:30). He was convinced that nothing could separate him from God's love in Christ (Rom. 8:38-39). He was positive that the gift of the Holy Spirit was a guarantee of final redemption (Eph. 1:13-14).

In short, Paul knew the comforting truth expressed by the Lord Jesus Himself that "of all [the Father] has given Me I should lose nothing, but should raise it up at the last day" (John 6:39).

So Paul was not talking about losing his salvation. On the contrary, as the context makes clear, he was talking about a race which could either be run victoriously or in which he might be "disqualified" from receiving a crown.

But could an apostle lose his crown and stand disapproved before his heavenly Judge? Yes, he could! Yet such a concept is barely appreciated today in some evangelical circles and is, on principle, rejected outright in others. "All Christians," we are told, "are overcomers." Disastrous Christian failure, resulting in significant loss of future reward, are alien ideas to much of contemporary theology. Rather, in these circles, catastrophic failure is thought to indicate an unregenerate condition.

But the New Testament is permeated by the concept that loss of victory is not inconsistent with true salvation. And the failure to recognize this fact has impoverished the church and clouded its perception of grace.

To put it simply, many of the New Testament warnings against failure and loss of reward are seen by many as warnings about the loss of salvation, or else they are taken as warnings against false professions of faith. In either case, the richness of God's saving grace is seriously minimized. At the same time lofty biblical motives for godly living are lost entirely from sight.

Faith and Works

Modern Christianity continues to wrestle with the issue of the relation between faith and works in Christian experience.[1] Many articulations of this relationship call into question the freeness of God's saving grace. The problems involved in understanding the New Testament doctrine of rewards are inseparably intertwined with the faith-versus-works controversy.

In a recent statement resulting from extensive Roman Catholic and Lutheran dialogue, it was agreed that while salvation takes place solely as an act of divine grace, the works that follow are also "necessary."[2] But logically this means that final salvation from hell depends on both faith *and* works. Accordingly, works are elevated to the level of a *condition* for salvation even if they are not seen as the *immediate cause* of salvation. This position is commonly admitted by classic Reformed theologians as well.[3]

At their core, all such systems of thought are "legalistic" in the broad sense of that term. They insist, in some way, on obedience to the "Christian law" as an essential element in the final escape from damnation. There is little room for a doctrine of rewards in such a system, since eternal felicity itself is a kind of "reward" which all Christians acquire. If a professing Christian fails significantly, he fails to attain the bliss of heaven itself.

It is foreign to such modes of thought to conceive of a God who unconditionally accepts the sinner without regard, not only to his past conduct, but also to his future conduct as well. And those who *do* conceive of God in these terms are stigmatized as "antinomian" (lawless).[4] It is as though the father of the Prodigal Son had been unwilling to receive that son back again without some guarantee from him that his future behavior would be better! But though the Prodigal had originally thought of asking to serve the father (Luke 15:18-19), he does not actually make the offer when he comes back (15:21). Nor does the father ask for it!

But many evangelists ask for it. They do this either by demanding repentance on the part of the sinner (in the sense of a decision to change his life),[5] or by insisting that saving faith carries with it an appropriate recognition of Christ's Lordship over the life, or in a variety of other ways. But all of these techniques are mere devices designed to extract from the sinner some kind of "commitment" to become a better person. Preachers who articulate the message in this way are blind to the unconditional grace of God. They are also regrettably imbued with that spirit which lies at the core of all legalistic modes of thought: that my fundamental acceptance before God must somehow be related to my conduct, that is, to my works.

That a man could be (as Paul was!) concerned that he might forfeit significant future reward, while all the while remaining sure that God's love would be his forever—that is a conception that defies the comprehension of many evangelicals today.

Faith Subtly Redefined

The result of the lack of perception just described has been an effort, on the part of many, subtly to redefine the nature of saving faith. This has often seemed a necessity, no doubt, because of the many texts which predicate eternal life on nothing more than faith.

When one reads, for example,

Most assuredly, I say to you, he who believes in Me has everlasting life (John 6:47),

how does one extract from this the concept of repentance, or submission to Christ's Lordship, or anything else other than simple belief? The answer is, of course, that this can only be done by rearticulating the notion of saving faith in such a way as to embrace more than simple trust.

The methods for doing this are many and varied. Thus we may hear of the distinction between "head" and "heart" belief. Or between "dead" and "living" faith (based on a faulty understanding of James 2). Or we may be told that biblical faith implies "commitment" or "a personal relationship" or something else. But in the end the result is that the simple biblical concept of "faith" or "trust" has become cluttered with all sorts of connotations that are foreign to the original New Testament word. No wonder many Christians struggle with the problem: "Do I have the right kind of faith?"

All efforts to import special content into the biblical words for faith are fundamentally unsound. They often involve a language error, which is increasingly well-recognized, called "illegitimate totality transfer."[6] This is a procedure whereby implications drawn from a context, or a number of contexts, are wrongly made to become part of the meaning of a word.

The fact is that the Greek expressions for "believe in" or "believe that" are not significantly different from their English equivalents. No one supposes that the English words "believe in" denote a "personal relationship," much less "submission to," or anything of that sort. Much pseudo-scholarship has been expended in an attempt to make the biblical concept of faith and trust carry the freight of a preconceived theology. The time has long since passed for this to stop.

Equally invalid is the well-known treatment of Acts 16:31. The words, "Believe on the Lord Jesus Christ," are often treated by those teaching a form of "Lordship salvation" as a call for submissive acknowledgment of Christ's Lordship as a condition for eternal life. But this is a glaring semantic fallacy.

If one says, "Put your trust in President Reagan," it is not semantically the same thing as saying, "Submit to the authority of President Reagan." In the first instance the title "President" simply presents Reagan as an authoritative figure who can probably follow through more effectively on his guarantees than can "private-citizen" Smith! In the same way, the title Lord used of Jesus presents the Savior as a divinely authoritative Person who can very well be trusted. To make more of it than that is to read one's own ideas into the text.

The attentive reader of John's Gospel will note that the expressions "believe in" (or, "believe on") are interchanged with "believe that." Thus we may read:

He who *believes in* the Son has everlasting life (John 3:36; emphasis added).

But we also read:

. . . but these are written that you may *believe that* Jesus is the Christ, the Son of God, and that *believing* you may have life in His name (John 20:31; emphasis added).

Thus it is clear that to "believe in," "believe that," and "believe" can all refer to the same act of saving faith.

From this it follows that to "believe in" Jesus is to believe something about Him—namely that He is the Christ.[7] What exactly this entails for John is made clear from a famous passage in the eleventh chapter of his Gospel. Here we find Jesus declaring to Martha,

> I am the resurrection and the life. He who *believes in* Me, though he may die, he shall live. And whoever lives and *believes in* Me shall never die (John 11:25-26; emphasis added).

This self-declaration is followed by a simple,

> Do you believe this? (John 11:26).

In response, John quotes Martha as uttering a statement of faith strikingly like his own thematic statement in 20:30-31. Martha replies,

> Yes, Lord, I *believe that* You are the Christ, the Son of God, who is to come into the world (John 11:27; emphasis added).

This tells us much about John's thought. For John, the "Christ" was the One who could make the claim of John 11:25-26 in which He guarantees the eternal destiny of the individual who believed in Him. To *believe that* He was the "Christ" was, in fact, to believe Him to be such a Person as that. It was to *believe in* Him as the Guarantor of one's eternal felicity and well-being. It was the "Christ" who guaranteed resurrection and unending life to the believer.

There is no room here for the subtle reshapings which some theologians have commonly given to the simple word "believe."[8] I either believe that Jesus is the Christ in the Johannine sense of the term, or I do not. But, by John's own statement, when such belief occurs, eternal life is thereby possessed. What could be simpler than,

> Whoever *believes that* Jesus is the Christ is born of God (1 John 5:1; emphasis added)?

It is precisely the loss of this pristine simplicity about the biblical notion of saving faith that has created enormous confusion.

When the word "belief" is subtly redefined, so as to ensure the sinner's commitment to good works, the result is an eclipse of the scriptural doctrine of grace.

In the half-light—or sheer darkness—that ensues there is little room for a viable doctrine of rewards.

CHAPTER

2

FALSE PROFESSORS

The question may be raised, however, how a doctrine of salvation through simple trust in Christ affects our conception of who is a Christian and who is not. Is it then no longer permissible to speak of false professions of faith, or of false professors? Is everyone a Christian who claims to be?

To ask that question is to answer it. Paul himself apparently believed that the Jerusalem church harbored people who were not genuine Christians. He thought of them, he tells us, as infiltrators of the Christian movement carrying on a "spying operation" in the interests of legalistic Judaism (Gal. 2:4-5).[1] But by so describing them—especially in the context of Galatians!—he makes it plain that he regarded them as hostile to his own proclamation of the grace of God. If they were not Christians, it was because they had in fact rejected the offer of divine grace.

Here, then, is one clear category of false professors. Those who claim the name Christian, yet have never bowed to the simple gospel of salvation by grace, have no right to that name. And by the same token those who believe themselves Christians but have

never understood the gospel offer must also be considered false
professors, however sincere they may be in their error. For one
cannot believe what one does not know or understand.[2]

Indeed, experience suggests that among the multitudes who go
forward in mass evangelistic campaigns are many who are
merely moved by the message, rather than actually converted by
it. Conversations with such people often disclose how little they
have comprehended the real nature of God's offer of eternal life.
And far too frequently it is the evangelist himself who has
clouded the issue.

It was not for nothing that the Lord Jesus Christ said to the
woman at Sychar's well,

> If you *knew* the gift of God, and who it is who says to you,
> "Give me a drink," you would have asked Him, and He
> would have given you living water (John 4:10; emphasis
> added).

After all, how was she to ask unless she knew what to ask for and
unless she knew Him whom she needed to ask? Saving faith is
thus not some blind leap amid the darkness of human ignorance.
It is the intelligent appropriation of a divine gift. It has been
aptly described as the hand of the beggar reaching out for the
divine benefit.[3] And the claim to being a Christian, without
actually receiving that gift, constitutes a false profession.

But those who speak of false professors often mean more than
that. Indeed, what is often meant are people who have apparently understood, and responded to, the terms of the gospel but
are thought to have an inadequate faith due to the lack of fruit
in their lives. But this conception is totally inappropriate and,
indeed, is subversive of the simple gospel of God's saving grace.
It is a conception that leads directly to the misguided efforts to
redefine saving faith that were described in the previous chapter.

The result is that many Christians are plagued by the question,
"Is my faith real saving faith, or am I a false professor?" The
turmoil which such a question can arouse can hardly be appreciated by those who have never encountered it in the Lord's
people. Those Christian teachers whose doctrines have been

influential in creating it will have much to answer for at the Judgment Seat of Christ.

And obviously, when a believer's appreciation of grace suffers so fearful an eclipse, it will be difficult if not impossible for him to build a life worthy of eternal reward when every rewardable effort is viewed as somehow a necessary evidence of true faith. It is only in the full blaze of God's unconditional favor and grace that the Christian will be able to focus, unhindered, on activities that will enrich his experience of the eternal future.

In short, the doctrine of eternal rewards is a clear stream only when it finds its source in the simplicity and magnificent freeness of the gospel offer. Sourced anywhere else, it is muddy, shallow, and ultimately ends in a dry bed.

The Narrow Gate

Ironically, perhaps the greatest utterance on the subject of false profession was made by our Lord in the midst of a passage which has been frequently, and at many points, misunderstood. The conclusion to the Sermon on the Mount (Matt. 7:13-27) contains more than one well-known piece of imagery and is often quoted. The solemn words of verses 21-23 are directly concerned with false professors, but they are best appreciated in the larger context of the conclusion as a whole.[4]

Following a summary of the morality on which His Sermon insists (Matt. 7:12), Jesus begins its conclusion with the familiar saying about the wide and narrow gates:

> Enter by the narrow gate; for wide is the gate and broad
> is the way that leads to destruction, and there are many
> who go in by it. Because narrow is the gate and difficult
> [lit., 'compressed'] is the way which leads to life, and
> there are few who find it (Matt. 7:13-14).

Many expositors read a text like this without reference to the larger teaching of the New Testament as a whole. But this is a mistake and an open invitation to read into it ideas which appeal to the interpreter but are foreign to its true meaning.

There is no good reason for thinking that these verses mean something radically different from our Lord's words in John 10:9, where He declares:

I am the door. If anyone enters by Me, he will be saved, and will go in and out and find pasture.

It would be pointless to ignore the transparent similarity between the statements of John and Matthew. Especially so, since both come from the lips of Jesus. In Christianity as taught by Christ, access to eternal life is available only on very restrictive terms. One only enters into this life *by faith*—and by nothing else!—by faith *in Christ*—and in no one else! No gate could be more narrow than that!

From the viewpoint of an ancient traveler approaching a Middle-Eastern city, the gate was a point of entrance. It is natural, therefore, that Jesus should employ this parable to encourage His hearers to find the right starting point for their spiritual activities. They need to be sure that they have found the entrance that leads to life. And that means finding the narrow gate and traversing the road ("way") which runs through it. Here, too, in the word "way" we hear another echo of Johannine thought (cf. John 14:6), for the Son of God is both the "gate" and the "road" that lead to life.

In contrast to this is the wide gate through which runs a broad road ("way"). Here man's liberal conceptions about the many ways by which God can be approached hold sway. This gate is thronged and crowded. It is the popular gate, a veritable marketplace of religious ideas. (Even first-century Judaism was multifaceted and rent by sectarian divisions!) Precisely for this reason Jesus must now caution about false prophets.

By Their Fruits

Few passages of the New Testament have been so grotesquely twisted as our Lord's warning about false prophecy. Misapprehension begins with its very first verse:

Beware of false prophets, who come to you in sheep's clothing, but inwardly are ravenous wolves (Matt. 7:15).

From this it should be transparent that false prophets do not give themselves away by their external behavior. In fact, they "dress" like sheep! That is, viewed from the outside they *seem like Christians*. They do not behave like the wolves they inwardly are.

But there is one key to their detection:

You will know them by their fruits (Matt. 7:16).

This famous verse has been woefully misread. As the previous verse should have warned us, it has nothing to do with the "life-style" of the false prophets. On the contrary, it has to do with their *words!*

This becomes unmistakable when Matthew 7:16-20 is compared with 12:33-35:

Either make the tree good and its fruit good, or else make the tree bad and its fruit bad; for the tree is known by its fruit. Brood of vipers! How can you, being evil, *speak* good things? For out of the abundance of the heart the mouth *speaks*. A good man out of the good treasure of his heart brings forth good things, and an evil man out of the evil treasure brings forth evil things (emphasis added).

Clearly both passages employ identical imagery, and Matthew 12 makes explicit a meaning which is required also in Matthew 7. A false prophet must be tested by his message. If he is inwardly corrupt and ravenous this will stand revealed by the character and quality of his communications. Men ought not to be deceived by his gentility, urbanity, or sophistication. They must reject such sheep's clothing when the spoken words expose the growl of a wolf!

It goes without saying, therefore, that this text has nothing at all to do with the alleged necessity of testing a man's faith by means of his works! It would be hard to imagine a text less suitable for that purpose than this one.

False Prophets/Professors

It seems clear that false prophets are still in mind when Jesus utters the words that follow. But now these men stand as a stark warning to any who might follow in their steps. Our Savior therefore declares:

> Not everyone who says to Me "Lord, Lord," shall enter the kingdom of heaven, but he who does the will of My Father in heaven. Many will say to Me in that day, "Lord, Lord, have we not prophesied in Your name, cast out demons in Your name, and done many wonders in Your name?" And then I will declare to them, "I never knew you; depart from Me, you who practice lawlessness!" (Matt. 7:21-23).

This is an arresting text, but it does not say what some have made it say. To begin with, it does not affirm salvation by works! Ironically, it is works that the false professors lay claim to. They have engaged in prophecy, exorcisms, and miracle-working in Jesus' name and yet are denied access to God's kingdom.

It must be remembered, moreover, that this is a scene set in a future day of judgment. These are not, therefore, conscious charlatans trying to deceive their Judge with bogus claims to miraculous activity! On the contrary, they are all too desperately sincere. Nor are their claims denied.

What *is* denied, however, is that they have a valid connection with their Judge, or He with them. "I never knew you" are His stinging words. And in this regard, as well, Johannine conceptions are relevant. Thus in John 17:3 Jesus declares:

> And this is eternal life, that they may know You, the only true God, and Jesus Christ whom you have sent.

Elsewhere He affirms:

> I am the good shepherd; and I know My sheep, and am known by My own (John 10:14).

These men are not His sheep, therefore, even if they did dress in sheep's clothing. They do not possess eternal life, otherwise He would know them and they would know Him.

They had not done "the will of My Father in heaven." But what was that? What did God want them to do in order to gain entrance to His Kingdom? Only one thing! (The gate is narrow!) He wanted them to trust His Son for eternal life. They had not done so. Whatever else they had done was irrelevant to their claims. And worse, it was "lawlessness" since it was done outside of a living relationship with Christ!

Matthew and John

But someone will object to this that we are reading John's theology back into Matthew. But why should we not? Were their theologies diverse? Let this diversity be demonstrated by those who think so.

On the contrary, the fourth Gospel is written with the avowed purpose of making salvation clear and accessible (John 20:30-31). Matthew makes no such claim. Indeed, the absence of explicit statements of the type which we meet everywhere in the Gospel of John (1:12; 3:15-16, 36; etc.) argues powerfully that Matthew writes for a Christian audience for whom the basic issues regarding faith and eternal life are settled and plain.[5] He can then presume that his readers will read such texts as this (Matt. 7:13-23) in the clear light of their knowledge of God's saving grace.

Regrettably, he could not have made the same assumption if he had been writing in our day! In fact, so clouded is the conception many Christians have of the gospel itself that if a text *can be* understood somehow as demanding obedience for final salvation, it *will be* understood that way! This lamentable situation—this eclipse of grace—has sadly distorted many of the passages in the New Testament which teach the doctrine of eternal rewards. It is precisely such passages that need to be recovered in all their edifying power.

CHAPTER

3

THE SERMON ON THE MOUNT

The Gospel of Matthew stands in impressive contrast with the Gospel of John in that Matthew reports an extended ethical discourse by Jesus rather early in His public ministry. In John, the even earlier discourses are private ones which deal with the issue of personal salvation. The two Gospels complement each other remarkably.

Both the conversation with Nicodemus (John 3:1-21) and the one with the woman at the well (John 4:1-26) took place before the Sermon on the Mount. We know this from the references in John 3:24 and 4:1 which show that John the Baptist was still active. In Matthew, in Mark and apparently in Luke, our Lord's public ministry commences after the Baptist is imprisoned (Matt. 4:12-17; Mark 1:14-15; Luke 3:20). This is of considerable importance.

What it means quite simply is this: that before Jesus undertook to become a public preacher, He had already indoctrinated His disciples in the basic truths of salvation. In John's Gospel we see that the disciples of Jesus have already become believers before the public ministry begins (John 1:35-51; 2:11). They are with Him as He evangelizes Sychar (4:27-42). There is no reason, therefore, why they should have construed the Sermon on the Mount—when they heard it—as furnishing an ethical formula for reaching heaven. That would have been to forget the simple gospel which they already knew quite well.

Yet modern expositors often forget that gospel when they read this Sermon! Indeed, they forget a great deal of the New Testament when they read it. Accordingly, when they read these words of Jesus,

> For I say to you, that unless your righteousness exceeds
> the righteousness of the scribes and Pharisees, you will
> by no means enter the kingdom of heaven (Matt. 5:20),

most interpreters overlook the Book of Romans. *Of course*, one cannot enter God's kingdom apart from a righteousness superior to that of the religious models of that day! (Jesus had not yet begun to denounce them publicly.) But what kind of righteousness is that? There is only one biblical answer to this question— the Pauline answer.[1] All righteousness is insufficient except the very righteousness of God which is imputed to men on the basis of faith alone (Rom. 3:21-26).

The words of Jesus are pre-Pauline!

Jesus and Paul

Once again the objection may be raised that it is inappropriate to read the words of Jesus through Pauline spectacles. But why? Paul himself claimed to have received his gospel directly from Jesus Christ (Gal. 1:11-12). Did Jesus never say anything during His public ministry that anticipated Paul's doctrine of justification by faith? It is highly improbable that He did not.

In fact, though it is hardly ever noticed, in the Sermon on the Mount as a whole, Jesus is doing something that is distinctly Pauline in nature. He is using the law as a means of convicting men of the fact that they are sinful.

The Sermon on the Mount had a double audience. On the one hand it was ostensibly preached to Jesus' disciples who were gathered before Him (Matt. 5:1). Technically, it was they whom He was instructing (5:2). From their perspective, the Sermon on the Mount can be understood as laying down the standards of conduct appropriate to a disciple of Jesus as he lives in anticipation of the coming kingdom of God.[2] Viewed from this angle, the Sermon contributes significantly to the doctrine of rewards.

But the Sermon had another audience as well. This was composed of the multitudes who followed our Lord (Matt. 4:25; 5:1). And Jesus never forgets their presence, even while he is prescribing a code of behavior for His own disciples. In fact, the Sermon on the Mount can be seen as a masterful interweaving of Christian ethics with preevangelistic activity.

To be sure, the Sermon contains no overt salvation text such as John 3:16. We cannot be certain, however, that in its uncondensed form it did not. As all would agree, Matthew 5-7 take only a few minutes to read, and the actual sermon must have been much longer. Matthew's condensation is what serves the purpose of his Gospel, and there is no good reason for thinking that Matthew's Gospel was not written with a Christian audience in view. Evangelism, then, was not one of his aims.

But perhaps the Sermon did not, even in its fullest form, get more specific about the terms of salvation than the portion which we actually have. If it did not, then what remains can be suitably called preevangelism. This is to say that the Sermon is neatly crafted to arouse in an unsaved hearer not only curiosity about the narrow gate to life, but also an urgent need to find that gate.

Jesus begins the Sermon on the Mount by describing the qualities of character which His disciples must cultivate (the beatitudes, 5:3-12) and by specifying the disciples' special role in the world (5:13-16). The two sections together constitute an introduction to the entire Sermon. By itself this introduction would be potentially convicting to an unregenerate man, who could easily perceive how contrary his inner impulses were to such lofty ideals.

The body of the Sermon (5:17-7:12) might very well be described as "Kingdom living." The standards of conduct which are here laid out are viewed from the perspective of the standards that will be enforced when the Kingdom actually comes. But these standards are nothing more nor less than the righteous demands of "the law and the prophets" raised to the highest power (cf. 5:17-18 and 7:12).

Thus, when the Kingdom appears, anyone within it who disobeys even its smallest demand and teaches others to do likewise, will have the lowest possible status therein (Matt. 5:19). Here, of course, it should be remembered that disobedience to the King will not be unknown during the millennium (cf. Zech. 14:16-19) and, in fact, this initial thousand years will be climaxed by a Satanically inspired rebellion (Rev. 20:7-10).

So strictly indeed will human relationships be governed in the Kingdom of God that a man can go on trial for unjustified anger with his brother or for calling him a numbskull (Matt. 7:22)! When harsher language than that is used, the offender may be liable to immediate banishment into Gehenna, the lake of fire (7:22). That, of course, is exactly the place to which the Beast and the False Prophet are banished (alive!) when the thousand years begin (Rev. 19:20). Unregenerate inhabitants of the Kingdom will be very numerous, as the final rebellion proves. But at any time, during the thousand years, the King may send any of them away to this abode of torment to await the judgment of the Great White Throne (Rev. 20:11-15).

Clearly, in every respect, the rod with which King Jesus will rule His realm will be a rod of iron (see Rev. 12:5; 19:15). The rebellious spirit of the nations will be shattered by that rod, and repressed, until it rises one last time under the guidance of Satan himself. This time, however, mankind's obstinate will is broken for good and forever.

Now this portrait of Kingdom righteousness is daunting even to the believer, but how much more so to one who thinks in terms of entering that realm on the basis of merit. And this was precisely how the typical Jew viewed that issue. Like Paul prior to his conversion, a religious Jew sought final acceptance before God through the righteousness which was in the law (cf. Rom.

10:1-4). What was such a Jew to think after hearing our Lord's exposition of all which that righteousness really entailed (Matt. 5:21-48)?

Conviction of sin and unworthiness was the only natural result. The Kingdom was a place where every jot and tittle of the law would be required (5:17-18). Indeed, the passing away of heaven and earth, to which Jesus refers, will occur only after the thousand years are over (see Rev. 21:1). In that millennial era, then, disobedience to the law's least demands, and the teaching of such disobedience, would result in the lowliest status which the Kingdom could confer (Matt. 5:10). But then, a hearer might think, what about disobedience to *many* of the law's demands *right here and now?*

Obviously, entrance into the Kingdom of God demanded a righteousness that was excellent indeed. In fact, said Jesus, it must be greater than that possessed by the scribes and Pharisees (5:20). But who could ever attain to a righteousness like that?

No one, Paul (the former Pharisee!) was later to tell us. For if a man did not acquire righteousness as a free gift, he could never be justified before God at all. But the law was designed to prepare men for this realization. Like a stern and demanding tutor it was intended to lead men to Christ (Gal. 3:19-24). By the law came—not justification—but the knowledge of sin (Rom. 3:20).

And no one ever used it to that end more effectively than Jesus did in His Sermon on the Mount. For if the exact nature of the righteousness required to enter God's Kingdom is left unspecified, at least the unsaved hearer is compelled to ask some searching questions about it. He is driven as well to think carefully about the narrow gate and to seek it diligently. Indeed, the tutorial role of the law of Moses, as Paul perceived that role, is superbly exploited in this Sermon by Him who is man's Tutor *par excellence.*

The Sermon and Rewards

The divine Tutor's skill, however, is not exhausted by this facet of His message. In fact, nowhere is the suitability of the Sermon on the Mount to its two sets of hearers more impressive than in its final paragraph (Matt. 7:24-27). In this conclusion to His conclusion (the larger unit is 7:13-27), the Lord Jesus Christ presents His memorable simile about the wise and foolish builders. The warning which He utters serves well as a solemn admonition to both saved and unsaved hearer alike.

The "life" which a man constructs—his "house"—needs an enduring foundation. But only the words of Jesus offer such a foundation. All else is unstable and shifting sand. In the great crises of life the floods and the winds of adversity test the stability of one's "house" and, if it is well-founded, the "house" survives. If not, it collapses in ruins.

The words come very forcefully to any unregenerate man in that vast audience. If his righteousness was not acceptable to God, if he had missed the narrow gate, then calamity lay ahead. If the convicting shafts had reached the target of his heart, he must inevitably sense that he was building on sand. The search for stable ground must begin at once.

But for the disciple there was an equally sobering thought. Though he had found the narrow gate and, by faith, passed through it on the restricted way, yet the question remained about how and where he should now construct his life's experience. And to this there could be but one answer for him also. He must build on the words of Jesus, for if he did not, calamity awaited him as well—not the calamity of eternal hell, to be sure, but calamity just the same.

Death, of course, is the ultimate storm. The survival of one's life experience, one's "house," is a pressing issue for all men, whether regenerate or not. The soul that must pass into eternity without Christ leaves behind a wreckage that is pitiful indeed. But so may a real Christian leave behind such wreckage. A life not lived on the firm foundation of divine truth invites disaster, no matter who lives it!

No wonder then that Paul strove to run a winning race and to avoid disqualification by his Judge (1 Cor. 9:27). No wonder he entertained the thought that the life's work of a man might be consumed by the flames of the Judgment Seat of Christ (1 Cor. 3:11-15). It is quite true that Paul taught justification apart from works. But he did not teach Christian living apart from works. Nor did he affirm that those works flowed inevitably from justifying faith. Instead, Paul instructed Titus:

> This is a faithful saying, and these things I want you to
> affirm constantly, that those who have believed in God
> should be careful to maintain good works. These things
> are good and profitable to men (Titus 3:8).

Here too, as we might expect, we meet the harmony between Jesus and Paul. The maintenance of good works is an effort—not an effort unassisted by God, of course, but an effort nonetheless. It is the labor of building a life that is securely founded on the rock of divine truth. It is good and profitable to construct a life like that. It is calamitous not to do so.

Thus the closing words of our Lord's first recorded public sermon are rich with implications about the life of a disciple. He must choose how and where to raise the edifice of his earthly experience. Built on the sand, that edifice will someday be rudely swept away. Founded on the rock, however, it will outlast every storm, including death itself.

By inference, then, this last kind of "house" is eternal. And a life that can be so described is clearly rewardable.

CHAPTER

4

THE INDESTRUCTIBLE LIFE

The vibrant note about living life which the Savior strikes at the end of the Sermon on the Mount is one that echoes clearly in His later public ministry as well as in the teaching of His closest disciples. But despite the significant role this theme plays in the pages of the New Testament, it is rarely appreciated in the modern church.

This is due, as usual, to the eclipse of grace. Passages which ought to have powerfully inspiring effects on Christian readers are reduced to statements about final salvation which square awkwardly (if at all!) with the simple gospel of God's saving grace. The confusion created thereby is devastating and deplorable.

In the language of contemporary Christianity the expression "to save the soul" has one meaning and one meaning only. It conveys to its hearers the concept of deliverance from hell. It is surprising, therefore, to discover that such a meaning has not the slightest scriptural warrant. To state it differently, the New Testament never speaks of the "salvation of the soul" in the sense of escape from eternal damnation.

As a matter of fact, in the Greek Bible as a whole (which includes the Greek translation of the Old Testament) the expression "to save one's soul" had chiefly the same significance which it had in ordinary secular Greek. It meant "to preserve the life."[1] But in the teaching of Jesus, this everyday Greek expression is raised to a new level of meaning which is pregnant with significant implications.

Saving and Losing the Life

In a memorable saying which is reported in all three of the Synoptic Gospels, and even reflected in John, the Lord Jesus issued a stirring challenge that was paradoxical in form. His words recorded by Mark were these:

> Whoever desires to come after Me, let him deny himself, and take up his cross, and follow Me. For whoever desires to save his life will lose it, but whoever loses his life for My sake and the gospel's will save it (Mark 8:34-35; cf. Matt. 16:24-25; Luke 9:23-24; and see John 12:25).

It is worth noting here that the Greek word rendered "life" is the same one which in similar expressions elsewhere is rendered "soul."

How such a declaration must have struck Jesus' contemporaries is not hard to imagine. Its hearers are variously described as "His disciples" (Matthew), "the people . . . with His disciples" (Mark), and "all" (Luke). Like the Sermon on the Mount this statement had a point for everyone, but must initially have seemed hopelessly perplexing. How could one preserve one's life and at the same time lose it? How could he lose it and at the same time save it? Can one die and live at the same time?

Of course our Lord was dealing in metaphor. One cannot *literally* both lose and save the life. But on a spiritual level things are different. On that level eternal realities come into play. From that vantage point one can speak of a life that is lost when viewed from an earthly perspective, but preserved when viewed from a heavenly one.

Conversely, one may speak of a life preserved from the standpoint of temporal experience, but lost from the standpoint of eternity.

Thus a martyr for the cause of Christ has certainly lost his life in a temporal sense. But the life laid down for God is not *really* lost. Indeed, such a life achieves a kind of immortality. Its value and impact are unending, as is also the glory it gains for the Christian who has made such a sacrifice.

On the other hand to shrink from the pathway of obedient suffering may be temporarily self-preserving. But the life thus selfishly held back is lost in terms of enduring eternal worth.

It would be a mistake to think here of heaven or hell. The call which precedes this challenging conception is a call to self-denial and bearing one's cross. It is a call to follow Jesus, that is, a call to discipleship.

Of course there are many who equate such a call with conversion, but by so doing they either explicitly or implicitly deny the freeness of the gospel. By no stretch of the imagination is the demand for self-denial and self-sacrifice an invitation to receive a free gift. The attempt to harmonize these polarities always ends either in hopeless absurdity or in theological sophistry.

In this respect the man on the street is often more perceptive than the theologian. If someone were to offer him a gift in return for self-denying obedience, he would readily recognize that offer as grotesquely misrepresented!

The Son of God never engaged in such contradictions. What was free, He represented as free. What was costly, He presented as costly. The experience here described is costly!

But it is also splendid. It is the construction of a life—a house—which can survive anything, even when it appears not to survive at all!

Of this fact our Lord's own experience is the superlative illustration. At the height of His ministry and public popularity, He is betrayed by a professed disciple and put to death by the Jewish and Roman authorities. It was a life apparently lost, a ministry apparently prematurely cut off. But as every Christian understands, it was the death of Jesus that gave to His life permanent and eternal worth. To have turned aside from the cross would have made that wonderful life spiritually valueless to all mankind. To have avoided this suffering would have frustrated God's purposes for that life.

The same truth, in principle, applies to the committed disciple. Indeed, in John, Jesus' way of saying this is instructive:

Most assuredly, I say to you, unless a grain of wheat falls into the ground and dies, it remains alone; but if it dies, it produces much grain [lit., fruit]. He who loves his life will lose it, and he who hates his life in this world will keep it for eternal life. If anyone serves Me, let him follow Me; and where I am, there My servant will be also. If anyone serves Me, him My Father will honor (John 12:24-26).

There is much to be learned from this way of putting it.

Losing one's life for God, we discover, is like the death of a seed of wheat. It is the secret of fruitfulness precisely because it is a life of service to Christ. The self-denial which this entails is now expressed in terms of "hating" our lives *in this world.* Instead of "loving" our lives—instead of guarding them selfishly for our own use—we abandon them to God's will. But in doing this we actually fuse our earthly experience into a continuum that stretches on into an unending future. We "keep it for eternal life"!

Or, to put it another way, the "house" we have built survives our physical death. It becomes an integral part of our experience in the everlasting world-to-come.

But the "house" which collapses in ruins is another thing altogether. In that case we encounter the *radical discontinuity* between the kind of living that is essentially temporal and that which is fundamentally eternal.

The Balance Sheet

It follows from this that no amount of temporal gain can possibly compensate for the loss of one's life. It is, therefore, no exaggeration for Jesus to inquire,

For what will it profit a man if he gains the whole world, and loses his own soul [= life]? Or what will a man give in exchange for his soul [= life]? (Mark 8:36-37.)

It is unfortunate that the familiar English rendering of these questions employs the word "soul." The continued use of "life" (found in verses 34 and 35) was much to be desired. The Greek word in all four verses is the same.

What Jesus is doing is computing the balance sheet of human experience. Suppose that in the column headed "gains" one could list "the whole world." And suppose in the column labeled "losses" one must write "my life." What, in that case, is the bottom line? Jesus' answer is stark and arresting. The balance sheet shows a net loss! The life is more valuable than anything that might be offered for it in exchange.

It is precisely this truth that is so tellingly expressed in the parable of the rich fool. After refusing to arbitrate between two brothers who were quarreling over an inheritance, Jesus says to the crowd around Him:

Take heed and beware of covetousness, for one's life does not consist in the abundance of the things he possesses.

Then He adds:

The ground of a certain rich man yielded plentifully. And he thought within himself, saying, "What shall I do, since I have no room to store my crops?" So he said, "I will do this: I will pull down my barns and build greater, and there I will store all my crops and my goods. And I will say to my soul, 'Soul, you have many goods laid up for many years; take your ease: eat, drink, and be merry.' " But God said to him, "You fool! This night your soul [= life] will be required of you; then whose will those things be which you have provided?" So is he who lays up treasure for himself, and is not rich toward God (Luke 12:15, 16-21).[2]

Here, if anywhere, we encounter the collapse of an apparently splendid "house"!

We are not told whether the rich man of this parable was saved or unsaved. Nor does it matter. The lesson which our Lord's story is designed to communicate would be true in either case. This man's life experience vanished the moment it was overtaken by physical death. The goods he was planning to hoard for his personal enjoyment, over the years to come, were totally lost to him. He left this world utterly impoverished!

Not surprisingly, Jesus follows this memorable narrative with an extended admonition to His disciples against an undue concern for the physical necessities of life (Luke 12:22-31). This warning is climaxed by urging them to give priority to the kingdom of God (v. 31), and He adds:

Do not fear, little flock, for it is your Father's good pleasure to give you the kingdom. Sell what you have and give alms; provide yourselves money bags which do not grow old, a treasure in the heavens that does not fail, where no thief approaches nor moth destroys. For where your treasure is, there your heart will be also (Luke 12:32-34; cf. Matt. 6:19-21).

And that was exactly the rich man's problem. His treasures were on earth and, inevitably, his heart was there as well. When he died, he left those treasures behind. He was not rich toward God.

But the disciples are urged to look at things differently. It is possible for them, Jesus declares, to store up heavenly treasure. It is possible for them, in other words, to be rich toward God.

Nevertheless, such wealth is not theirs automatically. On the contrary, it is something they are to *provide* for themselves (v. 33). Or, as the Savior had put it in His Sermon on the Mount, they were to *lay it up* for themselves (Matt. 6:20). This is what the rich man had conspicuously failed to do. The disciples must not follow his example.

It is evident, then, that the Lord Jesus Christ engages in a different form of accounting than men usually do. It was well for His unsaved hearers to know this, just as it was urgent that His disciples should know it. In the case of the former it could provoke them to reexamine their own values and begin to seek God's. And in the sincere pursuit of those things which counted with God, it was inevitable that they should ultimately find the narrow gate to life. In fact, in addressing doubters about His own Person, Jesus had once said, "If anyone wants to do His will, he shall know concerning the doctrine, whether it is from God or whether I speak on My own authority" (John 7:17). Indeed, it remains always and everywhere true that God is "a rewarder of those who diligently seek Him" (Heb. 11:6). So Jesus clearly thought it was well worth saying whatever might prompt an unsaved man to seek His heavenly Father.

But it was every bit as worthwhile for his disciples to hear this teaching, too. Moreover, as believers in Him, they could begin to act on it at once. They could begin at once to construct their "house" on the solid rock of their Teacher's words. They could commence immediately to lay up heavenly treasures for themselves. In short, they could cast their life into the soil of obedience to God—like a mere seed of wheat—and could look forward to a bountiful harvest. They could, in fact, save their lives by losing them!

That was what earthly life was really all about anyway. No wonder, then, that in Matthew's form of our Lord's saying there was a fresh and delicate shade of meaning: "For whoever loses his life for My sake will *find* it" (Matt. 16:25; cf. 10:39). One's life was not really *found* until it was discovered in self-denying service to Christ. And those who seemed to find it somewhere else—like the rich fool—had not found it at all. They had lost it![3]

It was solemn truth. And though it did not at all address the terms on which a man might be delivered from hell, it was still profoundly important. It was a warning that one's earthly life could be wasted, and heavenly reward could be forfeited, by misguided living.

And that was something *everyone* needed to hear!

CHAPTER

5

THE RICH YOUNG RULER

Rich fools, however, do not appear only in parables. They also appear in real life.

On one notable occasion Jesus met one. He was a wealthy young man, and his interview with our Lord is both familiar and classic. It was an interview that plainly disclosed the Savior's striking capacity to probe beneath the issues men raise—in order that He might reach the issues they *should* have raised.

The disciples as usual were with Him. And they stood to profit immensely from the exchange, which they are allowed to over-hear. Indeed, Jesus makes sure that they do profit by His direct dealing with the problems which the encounter raised for them. In the process He achieves—as He so often did—a double result.

On the one hand, He softens the ground in the young man's heart in order to prepare it for the seed of the simple gospel of His saving grace. On the other hand, He drives home to the disciples important truths about heavenly treasure.

The Young Man's Question

According to the account given in the Gospel of Mark, the interview began when the ruler reached Jesus on the run. Though he is only called "young" by Matthew (19:22), the eagerness of youth is apparent in this hasty form of approach. Perhaps, then, there was a breathless quality to his words when he said,

Good Teacher, what shall I do that I may inherit eternal
life? (Mark 10:17).

The question plainly reflects the typical Jewish perspective. According to common Jewish theology of that time, eternal life was a privilege that belonged to the age to come. Morever, it could be acquired only by those whom God deemed worthy to have it. The man's choice of the word "inherit" simply underscored this perception of things. That was a word which the rabbis often used to describe the meritorious acquisition of bliss in the future world.[1]

No wonder, then, that the young man thought he must *do* something to get eternal life. In fact, in Matthew's account the adjective "good" is added to the question: "What *good* thing must I do . . . ?" (Matt. 19:16.)

The Jewish outlook was both right and wrong. It was quite true that when eternal life was perceived as *an acquisition in the age to come* it could only be meritoriously obtained. In that respect Jewish thought was not misguided. But that was only half the story.

There remained a severe problem. Man was a sinner. He stood under divine condemnation. If he could acquire eternal life only at some future day—and only on the basis of his merits—then his situation was hopeless. He could, in fact, never acquire it at all.

But the coming of Jesus Christ into the world shed light on this issue in a fresh way. As Paul was later to say, He "brought life and immortality *to light* through the gospel" (2 Tim. 1:10). What was always latent in the Old Covenant revelation—what was there in shadowy form—was now brilliantly illuminated by the incarnation of the Son of God and by the gospel message which He proclaimed.

Now it was possible—such was the Savior's message—for a man to acquire the life of the age to come *immediately*. And not on the basis of merit at all, but as a free gift!

What else, indeed, did the Son of God mean when He declared,

> Most assuredly, I say to you, he who hears My word and believes in Him who sent Me *has* everlasting life, and shall not come into judgment, but *has passed* from death into life (John 5:24; emphasis added)?

Or again, when He went on to state,

> Most assuredly, I say to you, the hour is coming, and *now is*, when the dead will hear the voice of the Son of God; and those who hear will live (John 5:25; emphasis added)?

Staggering revelation! Resurrection, spiritually, at once! The life of the age to come possessed right here and now—by faith and nothing more!

But of this the rich young ruler knew nothing. His was not a wrong question to ask—it just wasn't the primary one. But that first question was one which he could not even guess.

No One Is Good But God

How then could he be moved in the right direction? What could deflect him from his preoccupation with merit? The response of Jesus could do that, if the young man would rightly hear it.

That response, however, must have sounded initially as if it had no connection whatever with the rich man's inquiry. No doubt he was even taken aback when Jesus replied:

> Why do you call Me good? No one is good but One, that is, God (Mark 10:18).

But nothing could have been more to the point. It was precisely the issue on which this man needed to focus.

He had addressed Jesus as "Good Teacher." No doubt it was glibly said no matter how respectfully it was intended. But was He *really* good? In the definitive sense of that word, He could not be "good" if He was a mere mortal man. The Old Testament bore witness to that fact (and Paul appealed to it!) when it affirmed, "There is none who does good, no, not one" (Ps. 14:3; cf. Rom. 3:12).

Only God was good and that could mean only one thing. Jesus could not be good unless He was also God. The young man perceived Him to be a teacher, and such He was. But He was very much more than that! And until the rich young ruler could hear His voice as the voice of the Son of God, eternal life—whether here or hereafter—lay beyong his reach.

But there was more. The young man himself was *not* good. Only God was good. But this perception also had not truly dawned on him, as his response to the Savior's next statement painfully shows.

His concept of "good" was therefore precisely his problem. That concept clouded his perception of Jesus, and it clouded his perception of himself. Until these perceptions were corrected, he was very far from God's Kingdom indeed.

You Know the Law

How could such correction take place? Ideally, it ought to have taken place by means of the law. Here, again, was the divinely appointed schoolmaster whose role was to lead men to Christ. By the law one could normally acquire the knowledge of his sin.[2]

Jesus says, therefore:

> You know the commandments: "Do not commit adultery," "Do not murder," "Do not steal," "Do not bear false witness," "Do not defraud," "Honor your father and your mother" (Mark 10:19).

To this list Matthew reports that Jesus even added, "You shall love your neighbor as yourself" (Matt. 19:19).

It ought to have been convicting. But it wasn't! Indeed, it actually elicits one of the most sanguine replies in all of religious history. The young man says:

> Teacher, all these things I have kept from my youth (Mark 10:20).

Had he? Of course not! What child is there who has *always* honored his father and mother? Where is the man who loves his neighbor as himself from his youth and upward?[3] Even if he had avoided the grosser sins on the list, he had certainly not avoided them all.

He was not good of course. But he *was* self-righteous! And like all self-righteous people he had lowered the standard of good to the level of his own imagined attainments. His darkness seems impenetrable.

One Thing You Lack

Yet there follows one of the loveliest statements of Scripture:

> Then Jesus, looking at him, loved him . . . (Mark 10:21).

How or why Jesus loved him is beyond our ability to fathom. But so is His love for all men—and for us. That love is mysterious, it is marvelous. It is not called forth by our deluded claims to goodness, nor is it deflected by our arrogant self-righteousness.

But it is our ultimate resource, "for God so loved the world that He gave . . . "!

It is, therefore, Jesus' love for this blind young inquirer which motivates our Lord's next words:

> One thing you lack (Mark 10:21).

What was that? The answer should be obvious to every Christian with a New Testament in his hands. The one thing he lacked was faith—saving faith![4]

No doubt it will be objected to this that it does not at all accord with the words of Jesus which follow immediately. But in fact it does accord with those words, properly considered. But not in the explicit one-to-one form which some readers inappropriately expect.

Here, too, the eclipse of grace casts its shadow over the interpretation of Scripture. Can anyone suppose that selling all and giving to the poor are really conditions for going to heaven? Were they even really conditions for this particular man? And if they are, or were, how can that conception of things be harmonized with the simple offer of a free gift of life to needy men?

"Whoever desires, let him take the water of life freely" (Rev. 22:17) is far from being identical with "sell whatever you have and give to the poor." Such declarations are manifestly not saying the same thing. Casuistry alone can reduce them to some form of equivalence.

No, this man lacked saving faith, just as does every unsaved man. He lacked the simple spirit of trust so characteristic of the little children Jesus had just received (see Mark 10:13-15). But the young man was not prepared just now to have his deficiency explicitly stated. He was much too self-righteous to feel the need for a Savior. After all, had he not said, "What must *I* do"?

Jesus did not believe in pouring water down a clogged hole. This man must be *prepared* to comprehend the thing he really needed. Shock treatment was clearly in order.

Thus it is that Jesus' challenge takes the form it does:

> Go your way, sell whatever you have and give to the
> poor, and you will have treasure in heaven; and come,
> take up the cross, and follow Me (Mark 10:21).

Clearly, this is a call to discipleship. It is an invitation to the utmost self-denial in the form of unstinting generosity.[5] Its outcome, Jesus declares, will be heavenly treasure.[6]

Was the young man prepared for this? Naturally not. In fact he goes away saddened since his wealth was considerable. But why did he go away? Above all, because he had more faith in his money than he had in Jesus.

Indeed, our Lord subsequently points this out to His disciples when He tells them:

> Children, how hard it is for those who *trust in riches* to
> enter the kingdom of God! (Mark 10:24; emphasis
> added).[7]

Let there be no mistake about it. The man lacked saving faith. No doubt when he asked what he might do to inherit eternal life, he suspected that his wealth might be tapped for some act or acts of benevolence. But it had not entered his mind that Jesus might ask him to surrender everything!

That he was unprepared to do, for then he would be surrendering the very thing in which he trusted: his money! He was clearly not ready to give up all that just on the *bare word* of this Teacher. And so he went sorrowfully away.

Life and Treasure

And that was a mistake. But it was a mistake Jesus knew he would make and which, in fact, conditioned the form of His challenge.

This man was confused about who was good. He himself was not good and his response to Jesus proved it. He was selfish, as are all sinners. For if he truly loved his neighbor as himself (as he had claimed to do from his youth), it would not have mattered to him whether he himself had his money or his neighbor. But it did matter. The rich young ruler was *not* good.

But Jesus was good, since He was God. If he were not God, His demand to give up all for Him was both fantastic and egotistical. Could a mere human Teacher talk like that and still be sane? How could a mere man offer eternal treasure to his followers on no other authority than his own? Would it not be foolish to trust an offer like that?

Ordinarily it would be. But not where Jesus was concerned. Yet such a leap of faith required the rich young ruler to adopt a much higher view of this rabbi than he currently held. Indeed, it required him to reach the conclusion that Jesus was exactly who He had hinted He was—a divine Person! And that meant that He was the Christ, the Son of God. But to reach *that* conclusion was to be born again, as the Gospel of John so plainly declares (John 20:30-31).

Did the rich young ruler ever reach it? He probably did, because Jesus "loved him" and had designed His words to meet this man at the very point where his spiritual progress was blocked.

All the implications were there. He now had reason to suspect that his own goodness was far less than he thought. And he had received unmistakable clues about the dignity of the Person to whom he had come.

All that remained was to believe in Him. That would have brought him the free gift of eternal life. Then he could take up the Lord's challenge to become a disciple. And *that* would have brought him treasure in heaven![8]

Aftermath and Surprise

The ruler was gone now, thwarted and dismayed by Jesus' words. Now it is the disciples' turn to be startled. Jesus says to them:

How hard it is for those who have riches to enter the kingdom of God! (Mark 10:23.)

And, to the disciples' amazement, He adds:

Children, how hard it is for those who trust in riches to enter the kingdom of God! It is easier for a camel to go through the eye of a needle than for a rich man to enter the kingdom of God (Mark 10:24-25).

The disciples are dumbfounded by these words, and they reply,

Who then can be saved? (Mark 10:26.)

Naturally, the disciples shared the common Jewish view that God enriched and prospered the righteous. There were many Old Testament examples of this: Abraham, Solomon, and Job, to name only a few. If salvation was hard for people like that, must it not be nearly impossible for those less signally blessed?

For a few moments the disciples themselves are tempted to lose their grip on the gospel of divine grace. (They were certainly not the last to be swayed in this way.) But there were no grounds for their perplexity if they considered Jesus' words with care.

Salvation was hard for the rich man precisely because he trusted in his own riches. He found it difficult, therefore, to feel totally dependent on Another, particularly on Jesus. The exchange with the rich young ruler had certainly demonstrated that!

It followed that a rich man was very much like an ungainly camel. He was too big, too self-sufficient, to pass through the minuscule entryway into the realm of eternal bliss. That, of course, was the narrow gate all over again. Only this time the image had undergone impressive miniaturization!

But the disciples need not worry, Jesus assures them. Salvation was always a miracle of God in any case. That which man could never bring to pass in the humblest of sinners, God could accomplish even in a rich man:

> With men it is impossible, but not with God; for with God
> all things are possible (Mark 10:27).

It was an important point. If we were to judge from the attitude of that wealthy young man, we might easily have said: "That man will never get saved!" From all appearances he was much too big a camel—much too proud a man—to ever become "small" enough to pass through the needle's eye by a childlike act of faith.

But it would be wise not to write him off entirely. Nor, for that matter, any other man of wealth. For what was truly impossible for human means to accomplish, God could do. Indeed, the masterly skill with which Jesus had handled the young ruler had no doubt set this miraculous process in motion. The camel had gone away smaller—less self-assured—than when he arrived. There was hope!

Life More Abundant

That ought to have set the disciples' minds at rest. Perhaps it did. In any case the focus of the conversation changes swiftly. Peter is the catalyst:

> Then Peter began to say to Him, "See, we have left all
> and followed you (Mark 10:28).

According to Matthew, he also added:

> "Therefore what shall we have?" (Matt. 19:27.)

It was an appropriate question. After all, Jesus had offered the rich young ruler *treasure in heaven* if *he* left all. Was this promise applicable to the disciples as well?

No doubt there is a temptation to censure Peter for greed. But why? Already the disciples had been specifically taught to store up eternal wealth (Matt. 6:19-21; Luke 12:32-34). It is not selfish to take an interest in matters Jesus Himself has told us to be concerned about. It is not wrong to seek what He tells us to seek.

It is wrong not to seek. It is, in fact, a sin to refuse to lay up heavenly treasure when we are explicitly commanded to do it. Moreover, the effects on our hearts of *not* doing it will be calamitous. For where our treasures are, there our hearts will be also!

The rich young ruler's heart was on earth. The thought of losing his earthly treasures saddened him. But Peter and the other disciples had abandoned everything for Jesus. It was only natural that they should be curious about their heavenly reward.

Our Lord's answer to this query is memorable:

> Assuredly, I say to you, there is no one who has left house or brothers or sisters or father or mother or wife or children or lands, for My sake and the gospel's, who shall not receive a hundredfold now in this time—houses and brothers and sisters and mothers and children and lands, with persecutions—and in the age to come, eternal life (Mark 10:29-30).

The answer was rich, exciting, and sobering. There were compensations to be experienced in the present age—along with its troubles—and there was compensation in the age to come as well.

With regard to the present age, the reward was to come in the form of rich personal relationships. And how often the servants of Christ have proved the truth of that guarantee! Leaving behind their earthly families, traveling often to the remote quarters of the globe, they have discovered *new* relationships created by the shared gospel of Jesus Christ. In those souls, therefore, whom they have won to Christ, in those to whom they have ministered the truth, they have found new brothers and sisters, new mothers and children. Homes have been opened to them and lands laid at their service as though they owned them themselves. And the depths of the spiritual communion established in this way with men have often seemed to be indeed a hundredfold more rich than those ties which Christ's servants have left behind. No doubt, in fact, it was in the spirit of these very words of Jesus that Paul greets "Rufus . . . and his mother *and mine*" (Rom. 16:13)!

But if obedience to Jesus enriched a man's temporal lot, it equally enriched his eternal one. And here the reward was . . . "eternal life"!

Yes, a reward! Plainly presented as such. But a reward belonging to the future age, not to the present one.

And thus Jewish theology was right—in part. Eternal life would be awarded meritoriously in a future day. What that theology failed to perceive was that, for such a reward to be within man's reach, eternal life must first be received as a gift.

Eternal life, be it understood, is no static entity, no mere fixed and unchanging object. Eternal life is the very life of God Himself, and as such its potentials are without limit. Had not Jesus Himself affirmed:

I have come that they may have life, and that they may have it *more abundantly* (John 10:10; emphasis added).

Yes, the possibilities were as infinite as the life itself. But to have that life *more abundantly*, one must first *have* it. To receive the enrichment of that life as a future reward, one must first accept it as a free gift.

The rich young ruler had put the cart before the horse. He had asked how to *earn* life before *receiving* it. He had inquired about God's rewards, before seeking His gift. Jesus had sought to push him back to the proper starting point, but one thing remained true. Leaving all for Christ *did* lead to heavenly treasure after all.

The rich young ruler was by no means ready to do that yet. The disciples had already done it. It was well for them, therefore, to hear about it. It was needful for them to discover that both present and future experience would be enriched and enhanced by their loyalty and commitment to Christ.

There was no need, then, to envy the rich young ruler at all. Perhaps he seemed to be far ahead of them in all respects. But the balance sheets of eternity could reverse that appraisal.

After all, Jesus assures them, "many who are first will be last, and the last first"! (Mark 10:31.)

CHAPTER

6

JUDGED ACCORDING TO WORKS

One of the men who received instruction from our Lord's exchange with the rich young ruler was the Apostle John. A special intimacy existed between him and the Savior, so that in the fourth Gospel he describes himself simply as "the disciple whom Jesus loved" (John 13:23; 19:26; 21:7, 20). It was he who leaned on Jesus' bosom at the Last Supper (13:23).

There is something lovely about the fact that a man so personally close to the Son of God should be selected to pen the Gospel which above all others discloses the free and unconditional love of God for sinful man. Indeed, in the Gospel of John we encounter the irreducible core of the saving message of grace, and in that message we hear the heartbeat of God Himself.

So, then, the One who had lain in the Father's bosom (John 1:18) shared these sublime truths with the man who lay in His! No one among men has ever understood these truths better, nor communicated them more clearly and simply, than the Apostle John. In fact, it is this Apostle, and no other, who reports to us a statement by Jesus that is breathtaking in its scope and impact. According to John, Jesus once said:

> Most assuredly, I say to you, he who hears My word and believes in Him who sent Me has everlasting life, and *shall not come into judgment*, but has passed from death into life (John 5:24; emphasis added).

This is certainly a splendid promise. It offers to the one who believes a most solemn guarantee that not only does he possess eternal life, but also that he need have no fear of judgment. Why? Because that experience is not for him: he "shall not come into judgment."

Yet, strangely, in the last book of the New Testament this same inspired writer reports another declaration of his Master which must seem to stand in tension with the earlier one. Here Jesus says:

> And behold, I am coming quickly, and My reward is with Me, to give to every one according to his work (Rev. 22:12).

It is true that the word "judgment" is not actually used here, but it is obviously implied.

It is also explicitly stated in other texts of Scripture. In his first epistle, the same author writes:

> Love has been perfected among us in this: that we may have boldness in *the day of judgment*; because as He is, so are we in this world (1 John 4:17; emphasis added).

And James, our Lord's natural half-brother, wrote:

> So speak and so do as those who *will be judged* by the law of liberty. For *judgment* is without mercy to the one who has shown no mercy. Mercy triumphs over *judgment* (James 2:12-13; emphasis added).

Naturally also, the Apostle Paul spoke of this event:

> For to this end Christ died and rose and lived again, that He might be Lord of both the dead and the living . . . . For we shall all stand before *the judgment seat* of Christ. For it is written: "As I live, says the Lord, every knee shall bow to Me, and every tongue shall confess to God." So

> then each of us shall give account of himself to God
> (Rom. 14:9-12; emphasis added; cf. 2 Cor. 5:10).

What then is this? On the one hand there is the solemnity of Jesus' promise that the believer does not come into judgment, and on the other hand the repeated apostolic declarations that he does. It goes without saying that the failure to sift this question through to an appropriate resolution, has been the source of considerable theological confusion and error.

Scylla and Charybdis

According to Greek mythology the navigational skills of ancient seamen were severely tested whenever they were required to sail the narrow passage of water between Scylla and Charybdis. Not a few ships, so we are told, were broken on the rock Scylla or sucked down into the whirlpool of Charybdis.

Nor have the vessels of contemporary theologians fared much better when called upon to steer a course through the scriptural channels which deal with judgment. On the one hand lies the danger of ignoring our Lord's guarantee that the believer is judgment-free. On the other hand the danger of minimizing the reality that he is not!

All of the biblical statements in question can be taken, of course, at face value. When Jesus declared the believer would not come into judgment, He was speaking in the context of eternal salvation. The believer has eternal life *already*. He has thus passed from death to life *already*. On that score, there is nothing left to decide, nothing left to judge.

There can therefore be no such thing as a judgment to determine whether a believer goes to heaven or hell. God has already handed down a definitive legal decision. Paul called that decision *justification*. The righteousness of God has been imputed to the Christian on the sole basis of faith alone.

That has nothing to do with our works, as the great Apostle affirmed when he wrote:

> Now to him who works, the wages are not counted as
> grace but as debt. But to him who does not work but

believes on Him who justifies the ungodly, his faith is
accounted for righteousness. (Rom. 4:4-5).

It follows then that those who believe in a final assize where the
believer's works will be brought to bear on the issue of his final
salvation—and many do believe in that—are believing a doctrine
which clashes fiercely with Pauline thought. To introduce the
issue of works is, for Paul, to introduce the question of merit and
debt.

But since God gives salvation freely to anyone who receives it
by faith, the case is closed before it can be opened. Nor will it
ever be opened. Or reviewed. The eternal destiny of everyone
who has passed out of death into life is settled forever. *In that
sense* there is no judgment for a Christian.[1]

But on the other hand, many who have perceived this magnificent truth have been reluctant to face the other texts of Scripture on this theme as directly and candidly as they should. There
is, in fact, no way to elude the reality that the believer does face
a judgment where his works—and hence the issue of "debt" and
"pay"—must be examined.

This is exactly what Jesus means when He declares, "My
reward is with Me, to give to every one according to his work"
(Rev. 22:12). The Greek word translated here as "reward" was
one which basically meant "pay" or "wages." Our Lord's meaning is transparent: "What a man has earned he will get."

There is no more lovely doctrine in Scripture than the doctrine of God's matchless grace. But in some quarters of Christen-
dom that superlative theme has been stretched almost beyond
recognition. It is perfectly true that grace will play a significant
role at the judgment of believers. Who has ever accomplished
anything apart from its enablement? But the Judgment Seat of
Christ is a place where the Christian's *performance* comes into
view. And therefore the question of merit comes into view as
well.

Not to maintain this balance with regard to the biblical doctrine of judgment is to invite—yes, to assure—the distortion of
much Scripture.

Accountability

There is urgent need, therefore, for a renewed recognition of Christian accountability. Not the kind of pseudo-accountability, however, which is so frequently hawked in the religious marketplace today.

The Christian is *not* in danger of losing his eternal salvation. Every believer in Christ not only has eternal life but will still belong to Christ when he is raised up at the last day (John 6:37-40). No one who has ever drunk of the water of life will ever be thirsty for that water again (John 4:13-14).

Neither is the Christian's accountability to be held hostage to a distorted presentation of the gospel or to some subtle reshaping of the concept of saving faith.

A Christian's accountability is just that. He is saved freely and forever by the grace of God. But once he has been saved he is profoundly responsible for what he does with the rest of his life.[2]

He can build his "house" on sand if he so chooses. But the "house" will collapse in ruins around him, and he will have to give an account of his folly before God. He can "save" his life if he chooses by self-interested living, but his life will actually be lost if he does. And he will have to give an account for this before God. He can hoard his material assets if he so decides, but to the degree that he does he will impoverish himself in the world-to-come. And he will have to acknowledge his greed before God.

Scripture is plain: "As I live, says the Lord, every knee shall bow to Me, and every tongue shall confess to God" (Rom. 14:11). That's accountability!

It is sometimes argued that the believer's sins cannot come under consideration at Christ's Judgment Seat since they are all forgiven. But this confuses the two kinds of judgment. The Christian's eternal destiny is not at issue in the judgment of believers, hence "sin" as a barrier to his entrance into eternal fellowship with God is not at issue either.

But it must be kept in mind that to review and assess a life, the Judge must consider the life in its entirety. And that obviously includes the bad with the good. Indeed, Paul tells us this quite plainly when he writes:

> For we must all appear before the judgment seat of Christ, that each one may receive the things done in the body, according to what he has done, *whether good or bad* (2 Cor. 5:10; emphasis added).[3]

That the thought was as solemn to Paul as it is to us is clear from his next words:

> Knowing, therefore, the terror of the Lord, we persuade men (2 Cor. 5:11).

Getting Ready to Meet the Judge

It behooves the Christian, therefore, to give the day of accounting some serious thought. It is an illusion cherished by many that unsavory secrets will always be just that—secrets between themselves and God. The Scriptures do not support this view of things.

Eternity has no secrets. Jesus Himself said so. In fact, while warning His disciples against the pretense so common among the religious leaders of His day, He said this:

> Beware of the leaven of the Pharisees, which is hypocrisy. For there is nothing covered that will not be revealed, nor hidden that will not be known. Therefore whatever you have spoken in the dark will be heard in the light, and what you have spoken in the ear in inner rooms will be proclaimed on the housetops (Luke 12:1-3).

The Apostle Paul carried this a step further:

> Therefore judge nothing before the time, until the Lord comes, who will both bring to light the hidden things of darkness and *reveal the counsels of the hearts*. Then each one's praise will come from God (1 Cor. 4:5; emphasis added).

It is too early, says Paul, to judge anything properly. To do that, one would need to know not only the dark secrets of men, but their *motives* as well. So wait until the Lord comes. Everything will be clear then! And when that happens, men will get whatever praise they truly deserve.

Therefore, since no human secret can remain a secret permanently, the Christian might well desire that the day of judgment should reveal more than "the hidden things of darkness." Why should it not also disclose secrets that are worthy of praise?

It will! And Jesus told us so in His Sermon on the Mount. In fact, one of His most motivating suggestions was this:

> But when you do a charitable deed, do not let your left hand know what your right hand is doing, that your charitable deed may be in secret; and your Father who sees in secret will Himself *reward you openly.*

Shortly after, He also said this:

> But you, when you pray, go into your room, and when you have shut your door, pray to your Father who is in the secret place; and your Father who sees in secret will *reward* you openly.

And a little later He added:

> But you, when you fast, anoint your head and wash your face, so that you do not appear to men to be fasting, but to your Father who is in the secret place; and your Father who sees in secret will *reward you openly* (Matt. 6:3-4, 6; 17-18; emphasis added).

What delightful secrets for a man to have—secret charities, secret prayers, secret fastings! Here surely are activities to be stored up in great quantity for that "day when God will judge the secrets of men by Jesus Christ" (Rom. 2:16).[4] And the reward for them—the "pay"—will be a recompense made in public!

That is one way for a Christian to get ready to meet his Judge. But there are other ways. In particular, as the thought of charitable deeds already suggests, one needs especially to be merciful. This was what James had in mind when he wrote, "For judgment is without mercy to the one who has shown no mercy" (James 2:13).

In saying this, of course, James was speaking to Christians who were to be judged by Christian standards, all suitably summed up as "the law of liberty" (James 2:12). He had been addressing them as people who held "the faith of our Lord Jesus Christ, the Lord of glory," but who tended to mix this with an inappropriate partiality toward the rich (2:1). This led to harsh, thoughtless, unmerciful behavior toward the poor (2:2-3), and was a serious infraction of the royal law of Scripture, "You shall love your neighbor as yourself" (2:8-9).

"All right then," James says, "just remember this. If you are an unmerciful person in your dealings with others, you must face a judgment that is not tempered by mercy!"

This was an arresting thought! For what Christian is there who can survey his earthly experience without sensing that, when called to account, he would wish to be treated with mercy? It is not a question of fearing the loss of salvation. That does not even enter the picture. But it is rather a question of being held strictly to the standards of God's Word and having our recompense measured out in those demanding terms alone. No honest believer wants a judgment exactly like that!

But many Christians are rigid and uncompromising in their demands on others. In addition, they can be thoughtless, unforgiving, unkind, and even cruel. And if this has been their manner on earth—if mercy has not marked their dealings with others—mercy will not mark their own judgment either!

So to get ready to meet his Judge, the Christian should specialize in mercy. After all, says James, "Mercy triumphs over judgment" (2:13).

But—and it is close to being the same thing—the Christian should also specialize in love. Mercy was James' word. Love is John's.

We should expect that love would be John's word. This was "the disciple whom Jesus loved." He had leaned on Jesus' bosom and felt there the heartbeat of God. He is preeminently the Apostle of love.

John believed firmly, of course, in the unconditional love of God, lavishly expressed in the giving of His Son that men might have eternal life. Naturally, there is no judgment ahead to test whether that love is still the believer's possession or not. A judgment like that is unthinkable!

But there *is* a judgment ahead to test the believer's works. "Behold, I am coming quickly, and My reward is with Me, to give to every one according to his work," are words recorded by the Apostle of love himself. John believed very deeply in that sort of judgment.

And he also believed that such judgment could be fearful. Like Paul he knew "the terror of the Lord" (2 Cor. 5:11). But though this *can* be fearful, it need *not* be. And the way to avoid the fear which that day could bring, is . . . *to love!*

This, in fact, is the burden of his exhortation in the fourth chapter of his first letter. And its climax is reached in the apostle's reference to the day of judgment as potentially free from fear:

> Love has been perfected among us in this: that we may have boldness in the day of judgment; because as He is, so are we in this world. There is no fear in love, but perfect love casts out fear, because fear involves torment. But he who fears has not been made perfect in love (1 John 4:17-18).

So that is it! As Christians enter a mature, perfected experience of loving each other, they no longer need to anticipate the day of accounting with trepidation. Why? Because they become like their Judge! "As He is" so we also may become in this world by love. Mature love expels fear when moral likeness exists between the Judge and the one who is to be judged.

There is torment in all fear, of course. Fear, in a sense, carries its own punishment with it. Though the believer can know himself to be eternally secure, this fact does not automatically eliminate the "torment" involved in anticipating the day of accounting. To stand before so majestic a Person (even John once fell at His feet as though dead: Rev. 1:17), to consider the standards by which our life must be assessed, to realize that much of it may meet with His censure and reproof—in all of that, and more, there are ample grounds for fearful anticipation.

But it need not be so, said John. Love can become the hall-mark of our temporal experience, just as it is the key to our eternal one. There is an irresistable logic to this correlation, and John stated it plainly:

> In this is love, not that we loved God, but that He loved us
> and sent His Son to be the propitiation for our sins.
> Beloved, if God so loved us, we also ought to love one
> another (1 John 4:10-11).

The saving, propitiatory work of Jesus Christ was an outflow of the unconditional love of God to men. By it, every believer is delivered from all judgment that would decide his eternal destiny in heaven or hell.

But that love is now a model for our love to one another. And when we really live that model we are then prepared to be judged without fear—according to our works!

CHAPTER

7

TEN CITIES

This distinctively "Christian judgment," to which the New Testament writers refer so often, is a theme whose roots are found in the teachings of Jesus. And that is precisely what we should expect. In fact, it is doubtful whether any major truth expounded in the Epistles is entirely absent from the recorded words of our Lord.

It was the Lord Jesus Christ, therefore, who first taught His disciples the reality of Christian accountability. Indeed, when the pages of the Synoptic Gospels are carefully searched, it is even surprising how extensively He dwelt on this subject. This fact goes unrecognized only because the first three Gospels are usually read today in the half-light of the eclipse of grace.

It is precisely the theme of accountability that underlies our Lord's teaching about saving or losing one's life. The loss of one's life, said Jesus, was a forfeiture for which there could be no adequate compensation:

> Or what will a man give in exchange for his soul [= life]?
> (Mark 8:37).

It is not surprising, then, to find these words immediately followed by a solemn reference to the future:

> For whoever is ashamed of Me and My words in this
> adulterous and sinful generation, of him the Son of Man
> also will be ashamed when He comes in the glory of His
> Father with the holy angels (Mark 8:38).

It should be seen that there is nothing here about the loss of eternal life. On the contrary, what is suggested plainly is the loss of honor and recognition in the glorious presence of Jesus Himself when He returns to reign. For what could be more honorable than to gain His approval in that day? And what could be more shattering to a child of God than to become the object of his Lord's embarrassment and shame?

Naturally, if *He* is ashamed of us, *we* will be ashamed of ourselves. And this possibility was pointedly expressed by the Apostle John when he wrote:

> And now, little children, abide in Him, that when He
> appears, we may have confidence and *not be ashamed*
> before Him at His coming (1 John 2:28; emphasis added).

It is often overlooked that the experience of shame described in this text belongs to a *transformed believer!* John says quite clearly, in the next chapter, that "when He is revealed, we shall be like Him, for we shall see Him as He is" (3:2). But the possibility of shame is not eliminated by the fact that the sight of our Lord will be transforming. Instead, that transforming sight increases this possibility.

Shame, when it has a valid basis in our behavior, is always experienced in direct proportion to our sensitivity to sin. But so long as we are in our mortal bodies, deep shame over spiritual failure is greatly inhibited by the sinful side of our nature. But not so in the bodies we are destined to have at the Second Coming.

In those bodies, transformed so that they are like the Savior's own glorious body (Phil. 3:20-21), we will be able to see things as they really are. In them we shall know even as we are known (1 Cor. 13:12). At that moment the capacity to feel holy shame over a life badly wasted will be for the first time unfettered by our excuses and rationalizations. Such shame will undoubtedly be more intense than any similar feelings experienced on earth.

Solemn thought! The Son of God and His redeemed child face to face at last. And if *He* feels shame toward us, those feelings will be mirrored in our own!

But if shame in the presence of Jesus were our only concern about the day of accounting, it would probably not be adequate to motivate our often calloused hearts. It is perfectly true that we ought to zealously seek to avoid both His shame and our own. But there is more to be avoided than that.

For this reason, the Lord Jesus told several vivid parables designed to bring the day of Christian judgment graphically before our minds. Each of them is rich with instruction and worthy of attention. But one of the clearest and most compelling is the parable of the ten minas. It is to this parable that we must turn our attention first of all.

The Prospect of Power

The parable of the minas was evidently told in the household of Zacchaeus (see Luke 19:11). This notorious publican had just been saved, and in the first flush of salvation joy had announced his intention to engage in lavish charity and in acts of restitution (19:8). The parable is designed to encourage him in this course of action.

It should be pointed out that Zacchaeus' willingness to dispose of large sums of money was no more a means to his salvation than it was for the rich young ruler. Nor does Jesus even refer to it when He proclaims the advent of salvation in that household. Instead He says:

> Today salvation has come to this house, because he also
> is a son of Abraham; for the Son of Man has come to
> seek and to save that which was lost (Luke 19:9-10).

The earliest Christian readers for whom Luke was writing no doubt understood Jesus' words quite well. If, as seems likely, they were Pauline Christians, they would detect at once the rich connotations of the expression "son of Abraham."[1] After all, it was Paul who wrote:

> Therefore know that *only* those who are of faith are sons of Abraham (Gal. 3:7; the translators have supplied "only").

What our Lord meant, therefore, was that salvation had come to Zacchaeus precisely because he was now truly a son of Abraham by faith. Jesus' irony would be unmistakable in Jericho where Zacchaeus must have seemed less than a real Jew: Zacchaeus had been a tax-gatherer for the hated Roman overlords. But Zacchaeus had simply been lost and, because Jesus had sought him, he was now found. Like anyone else, he had been saved by the kind of justifying faith of which Abraham was the great prototype.

Yet Jesus knew that Zacchaeus needed new incentives for his fledgling Christian life. In Jericho this man, who was short in stature, stood tall in terms of personal power. He was not only a tax-gatherer, he was the *chief* tax-gatherer in that city (19:2). And he was rich. There was probably no one else in Jericho who could rival him in his capacity to exercise influence and authority.

But now his stature in the city was about to be diminished by an extensive redistribution of his personal wealth. Might he not someday regret this resolution? Might he not someday see it as a rash decision made in the midst of an immature enthusiasm?

Jesus wanted to make sure he did not. Zacchaeus' public pledge to his new-found Master was the most prudent financial investment he had ever contemplated. Perhaps it would indeed diminish his influence in Jericho. But that did not matter. Jericho was but one relatively small Palestinian city—Zacchaeus should now aim for ten cities!

Thus the desire for power that evidently motivated Zacchaeus in his unsaved days could now be channeled in a new—and holy—direction.

It should not be forgotten that man certainly was created for the exercise of power. This is plain from the very first chapter of Genesis:

> Then God said, "Let Us make man in Our image, according to Our likeness; let him have dominion over the fish of the sea, over the birds of the air, and over the cattle, over all the earth and over every creeping thing that creeps on the earth" (Gen. 1:26).

It was undoubtedly of this text that the psalmist was thinking as he declared:

> What is man that You are mindful of him, and the son of man, that You visit him? For You have made him a little lower than the angels, and You have crowned him with glory and honor. You have made him to have dominion over the works of Your hands; You have put all things under his feet, all sheep and oxen—even the beasts of the field, the birds of the air, and the fish of the sea that pass through the paths of the sea (Psalm 8:4-8).

Man surely was created in the image of God. But the God in whose image he was created is a God of might and dominion. He is the King of glory to whom belong the earth and "all its fulness" (Psalm 24). Thus, as a true reflection of his Maker, man was designed to exercise dominion over the creation.

But he lost this dominion by his fall! And his former position can only be recovered in and through our Lord Jesus Christ Himself. For this reason the writer of Hebrews applies Psalm 8 to "the world to come" (Heb. 2:5) and to the destiny of Jesus (2:8-9) and to the destiny of the "many sons" (2:10).

Consequently, there is nothing wrong with man's urge to possess power, insofar as this drive is properly focused on God's purposes in creation. But power, like all legitimate human aspirations, is subject to the corrupting impact of man's fallen state. Zacchaeus had previously sought power in a way that reflected his sinful condition. Now he must learn to seek it as a high and holy ambition which was focused on the world to come.

A *Time for Investment*

There was another reason for the parable told by Jesus in the house of Zacchaeus. He was close to Jerusalem, and many of those who followed Him were anticipating that God's Kingdom would immediately appear (Luke 19:11).

This was a mistake. A period of time would elapse before the advent of God's reign on earth. The future King—our Lord Himself—would soon depart and go back to heaven, and only thereafter would He return to rule. Of Him, therefore, it could be said:

A certain nobleman went into a far country to receive for himself a kingdom and to return (Luke 19:12).

The procedure was familiar to His hearers. A man of noble birth might go to Rome, the center of imperial power, and seek the Imperator's approval of some claim to client kingship in a distant province. Indeed, it was by a process much like this that Herod the Great had secured recognition as king of Judea. He later asserted that claim by force of arms.[2]

But Jesus would carry His case to a Throne that was higher than Caesar's. And in accordance with a Psalm that prophesied His unqualified acceptance before the Ruler of the Universe, God would say to Him:

Sit at My right hand, till I make Your enemies Your footstool (Psalm 110:1; see Luke 20:41-44 and parallels; Heb. 1:13).

His enemies, therefore, were doomed. Their efforts to frustrate His claims (Luke 19:14) could only end in their own destruction (19:27).

But what about His servants? Here lay the central point of the parable. The interadvent period which the parable proclaimed could be used to advantage. It was a time for investment. More than that, it was a time for investment directly related to the coming Kingdom of God.

Therefore, Zacchaeus needed to hear the parable at this crucial moment in his life. But so did everyone else in the audience as well.

What was there to invest? For each servant it was a mina—a piece of money. Zacchaeus, the tax-collector, could appreciate a story about money! And it was no insignificant piece of money at that. It was an amount which an ordinary working man might accumulate only after about three months of labor. Yet, in the light of the potential return, a mina was not very much after all!

Each servant received the same amount—*one* mina. This suggests that our Lord was thinking of the one thing all His servants have in common: their life's potential. Whatever may be their differences in aptitude or situation, all had a life that could be invested with all its potentialities for Him. The echoes of His great saying about saving or losing one's life are thus not difficult to detect in the background of this story.

But though each of the ten servants *began* with the same amount, they do not all *end* with the same amount! This fact became evident on the day of accounting. Accordingly we read:

And so it was that when he returned, having received the kingdom, he then commanded these servants, to whom he had given the money, to be called to him, that he might know how much every man had gained by trading (Luke 19:15).

There is no mistaking here the Judgment Seat of Christ. This is a judgment of servants which, in this parable, is set in sharp contrast to the later judgment of enemies. The enemies of the King are slain (19:27); none of the servants are!

Given, therefore, the parabolic form of our Lord's instruction, it is not hard to see in the death of these enemies a reference to the Judgment of the Great White Throne which terminates in "the second death" for the unsaved (Rev. 20:11-15). But this judgment is removed by a thousand years from the advent of the King. No believer in Christ need fear such a judgment. It is something into which believers cannot come (John 5:24).

But the day of accounting *for servants* is clearly another thing. Their use of their life—the investment of their mina— must be reviewed. And all do not fare equally well!

Sharing the Kingdom

The first servant has invested his mina with remarkable profit. Its value has increased 1,000 percent. He now has *ten* minas to present to his Lord (Luke 19:16).

His reward is according to his work (Rev. 22:12). The King replies:

Well done, good servant; because you were faithful in a
very little, have authority over ten cities (Luke 19:17).

This was a splendid recompense! For the prudent investment of a sum earnable in a relatively short span of time, this diligent servant is elevated to a role of high authority in the new King's domain. He receives ten cities!

Zacchaeus must not miss this truth. The Guest whom he had received under his roof was the future King of all mankind. If Zacchaeus invested his life and its resources as well as his initial commitments suggested he might, he could actually share the power of God's coming Kingdom. And he could share it on a scale that was commensurate with his own dedication to the King.

The second servant, however, has used his life's potential less well. Still, he has earned a significant return on his Lord's investment. He has earned five minas. To him, therefore, the King replies:

You also be over five cities (Luke 19:19).

A thought-provoking response indeed! This time there was no "well done" as there had been for the first servant. There had been no explicit reproof either. And there was a significant reward. Clearly, this servant was a "middle man" whose life merited neither unqualified praise nor sweeping rebuke.

Zacchaeus should ponder this. His commitment to generosity had been wonderfully open-handed. Let him beware lest a tendency to retreat from this should diminish the ultimate value of his investment.

Why should he aim for only five cities? Why not aim for the unstinting praise of his new-found Lord and Master?

But there was another servant. He had done nothing with his mina, except to wrap it in a cloth and hide it (19:20). His excuse for this was his fear of the severity of his Master. His was a Master who did not concern Himself only with His own activities. He was concerned with that of others as well. He expected to collect what he had not personally deposited and to reap what He had not personally sown. Clearly, He was a demanding Lord (19:22).

To this timid figure the King replies:

> Out of your own mouth I will judge you, you wicked servant. You knew that I was an austere man, collecting what I did not deposit and reaping what I did not sow. Why then did you not put my money in the bank, that at my coming I might have collected it with interest? (Luke 19:22-23).

The excuse made by the unproductive servant was invalid. His fearful recognition that his Lord expected gains from the efforts of others should have driven him to the appropriate activity.

But it had not. Like Paul, he knew "the terror of the Lord," but unlike Paul this did not spur him to service (2 Cor. 5:11).

His Master now turns solemnly to those standing around Him. (This is no private audience, but a public one!) His words are sobering.

> And he said to those who stood by, "Take the mina from him, and give it to him who has ten minas."
> (But they said to him, "Master, he has ten minas.")
> For I say to you, that to everyone who has will be given; and from him who does not have, even what he has will be taken away from him (Luke 19:24-26).

Life's opportunity had been lost! The mina was gone. It was put into the hands of the faithful servant whose opportunities, now represented by *ten* minas, are augmented even further.

The wicked, slothful servant had nothing to show for the opportunity he had been given. So even the opportunity itself is taken away from him. A Kingdom had come where the possibilities for serving the King were richer and more varied than anything one had ever known before. The man who had served well with his one mina now found a fresh and challenging door opened to him. He could now serve his Master more fully by ruling ten cities for Him.

The unfaithful servant found that same door closed—decisively and completely.

No doubt it would be embarrassing. But it would be much more than that! In that moment when a servant of Christ might long more genuinely than ever for the chance to do something significant for His Savior, the golden portal into such service was barred forever. The Christian was face to face with the Master who loved him—and whom he had failed! The cost in wasted potential was staggering.

Zacchaeus could think about that if he were ever tempted to renege on his new commitment to generosity. A return to selfish living was the most imprudent step he could possibly contemplate.

To do that would be to wrap his mina in a handkerchief. To do that would be to throw his life completely away.

Hopefully, he never seriously considered that option at all.

CHAPTER

8

TO RECEIVE A KINGDOM

In a real sense, the King had "denied" his unfaithful servant.
He had denied him approval and given him rebuke instead. He
had denied that servant the opportunity to serve and had given
the opportunity to another instead.

This truth had deeply ingrained itself in the thinking of the
early church, and found expression in a nicely crafted "faithful
saying" designed to admonish Christians. Paul spoke of it in his
second letter to Timothy:

This is a faithful saying:
For if we died with Him,
    We shall also live with Him.
If we endure,
    We shall also reign with Him.
If we deny Him,
    He also will deny us.
If we are faithless,
    He remains faithful;
He cannot deny Himself (2 Tim. 2:11-13).

Much Christian truth is wrapped up in these pithy, memorable expressions. Very neatly they balance Christian certitudes with Christian responsibilities.

To one who knew Pauline thought, as Timothy certainly did, it was clear that all Christians had died in spiritual union with Christ and were thus destined to live with Him. Truly, they could already do so as their oneness with Him was realized in personal experience (Rom. 6:3-9; Gal. 2:20). But their eternal future was sure: they would "live together with Him" (1 Thess. 5:9-10).

Equally certain was the truth formulated at the conclusion of the faithful saying. If we Christians were "faithless," this in no way affected His loyalty to us. Every guarantee that had been made to us in grace would still be ours, regardless of our lack of faith or fidelity. (The Greek word for "faithless" covers both possibilities.) "The gifts and the calling of God" were still "irrevocable" (Rom. 11:29).

For Him to act otherwise toward us, whatever form our faithlessness might take, was unthinkable. Our Lord always remained faithful to us precisely because anything else would be an act that "denied" His own nature and character. As the prophet had said long ago:

Righteousness shall be the belt of His loins, and faithfulness the belt of His waist (Isa. 11:5).

But between these two pillars of certainty ("we shall live with Him" and "He remains faithful") lay two alternatives that were fully conditional.

Since it was quite conceivable that we could be "faithless," it was also conceivable that we might not "endure." But if we did not endure, neither could we reign with Him.

In like fashion, a failure to endure could become a form of denial. There was, in fact, more than one way of "denying" one's Master. The denial could take a verbal form and involve an unwillingness to confess Him and identify with Him before men. Or one could deny Him by works that were unsuited to a Christian profession (Titus 1:16).

In either case, however, our denial would be appropriately recompensed by His denial of us. Not, of course, a rejection of our status before Him as redeemed and justified people. *That kind* of denial would touch the question of His own faithfulness.

But the kind of denial experienced by the unfaithful servant in the parable of the ten minas was all too solemn a possibility. This was not a rejection of this man's position in the family of God. It was rather a rejection of his role *as a servant*. Since that role had not been carried out during his earthly life, it could not be carried out in the Kingdom either.

In short, the unproductive servant was not allowed to reign with His Lord. That priceless privilege of service was denied to him. He was judged according to his works!

Heirs of the Kingdom

It should be obvious that the faithless servant of our Savior's parable was not an heir of the Kingdom of God. It *should* be— but to many it is not.

Here again the shadow cast by the eclipse of grace has darkened many Scriptures that would otherwise be clear and plain. To many of the Lord's people, when one speaks of "inheriting" the Kingdom one is only talking about *getting into it*.[1]

Few equations are more gratuitous and superficial. Why should "inherit" equal "enter"? There is no good reason. Purely on the grounds of ordinary usage, "entering a house" or even "living there" are not the same as "inheriting a house." The latter speaks of ownership in a way that the former does not.

Nor was biblical usage any different. In normal Old Testament usage an "inheritance" referred especially to property that one owned, particularly what was passed down through a family or a tribe.

Thus we may note that the property that had belonged to Zelophehad of the tribe of Manasseh—which is called his "inheritance" (Num. 36:2)—had been passed to his five daughters in the absence of any sons. But their "inheritance" was safeguarded for the tribe of Manasseh by the Mosaic stipulation that the daughters must marry within their own tribe. Hence Moses laid down a rule that was binding on all the tribes and safeguarded the tribal properties:

> So the *inheritance* of the children of Israel shall not change hands from tribe to tribe, for every one of the children of Israel shall keep the *inheritance* of the tribe of his fathers. And every daughter who possesses an *inheritance* in any tribe of the children of Israel shall be the wife of one of the family of her father's tribe, so that the children of Israel each may possess the *inheritance* of his fathers. Thus no *inheritance* shall change hands from one tribe to another, but every tribe of the children of Israel shall keep its own *inheritance* (Num. 36:7-9; emphasis added).

"Inheritance" and "property," then, were often convertible ideas. To inherit was thus to "own" or "possess."

There was, moreover, nothing strange about the concept of "living" in a land where one had no "inheritance" or property. Thus the Old Testament speaks frequently of the "strangers" who "sojourned" among the people of Israel. If a "stranger" underwent circumcision he could even be treated as a "native of the land" (Exod. 12:48-49), but the Old Testament does not speak of such people as having an "inheritance," since property rights were assigned to the Israelite tribes themselves.

Similarly, the Levites are expressly forbidden to own property in the land:

> Then the Lord said to Aaron: "You shall have no *inheritance* in their land, nor shall you have any portion among them; I am your portion and your *inheritance* among the children of Israel" (Num. 18:20; emphasis added).

Shortly afterwards, we read:

> For the tithes of the children of Israel, which they offer up as a heave offering to the Lord, I have given to the Levites as an *inheritance*; therefore I have said to them, "Among the children of Israel they shall have no *inheritance*" (Num. 18:24; emphasis added).

From all this it is clear that, while "inheritance" is a multi-faceted concept in the Old Testament, one could easily speak of people living within Israel's territory without their having an "inheritance" there.

In the same way, there is no difficulty at all in speaking of people who *live* in the Kingdom of God but who do not *inherit* that Kingdom. Indeed, we *must* so speak as is proved by a decisive statement of Paul. In his famous discussion of the resurrection, the Apostle writes:

> Now this I say, brethren, that flesh and blood *cannot inherit* the kingdom of God (1 Cor. 15:50; emphasis added).

In the context this can only mean that mortals who do not possess transformed or resurrected bodies are barred from *inheriting* God's Kingdom. But this cannot be synonymous with being prohibited from *living there.* Otherwise one could not account for the great, unregenerate multitude which follows Satan in his final rebellion at the end of the thousand years. This host, in fact, is all too mortal, for they are "devoured" by the fire that descends on them from heaven (Rev. 20:7-10).

Paul does not intend to say, therefore, that human beings in mortal bodies cannot *live* in God's Kingdom. Rather, in line with the very basic sense of "inheritance" as that which one "owns" or "possesses," Paul means that only people in immortal bodies can "possess" this Kingdom. And that's different!

Of course, neither does Paul say that *all* transformed or resurrected people inherit the Kingdom of God. That is not true either. What he does affirm, however, is that this inheritance cannot be attained by mere mortal "flesh and blood."

The heirs of the Kingdom, then, are its owners, not merely its residents or citizens. And they are, without exception, glorified people who have acquired immortality. Immortality is thus a condition, but not the only condition, for inheriting God's Kingdom.

Meritorious Heirship

It is perfectly true, of course, that all Christians are God's heirs precisely because they are God's children. This fact is plainly stated by Paul (Rom. 8:17a). But the biblical conception of heirship is not the facile, simplistic notion that is so often suggested.

Without question, all Christians will "inherit" resurrection life. That is their birthright, as Jesus Himself affirmed:

And this is the will of Him who sent Me, that everyone who sees the Son and believes in Him may have everlasting life; *and I will raise him up at the last day* (John 6:40; emphasis added).

And, of course, this immortality consists in a sinless and glorious likeness to Christ. Thus Paul declared:

For whom He foreknew, He also predestined to be conformed to the image of His Son, that He might be the firstborn among many brethren. Moreover whom He predestined, these He also called; whom He called, these He also justified; and whom He justified, these He also glorified (Rom. 8:29-30).

These are impressive words and, as often stated, there is no break in this chain. Those who are predestined to conformity to Christ are not only called and justified, but ultimately glorified as well. This is the child of God's inalienable inheritance.

But Paul's words also show that the Lord Jesus Christ is viewed as "the firstborn among many brethren" (Rom. 8:29). And every Jew instructed in the Old Testament law of inheritance knew well that the firstborn son received a "double portion" of his father's inheritance (Deut. 21:15-17). The idea that one son might inherit more than another son was thus commonplace in Jewish thought.[2]

If, then, we ask who owns or possesses God's Kingdom, the primary answer must be: Jesus does! He is its King. The Kingdom is *His* inheritance above all. Accordingly, speaking of David—and of David's greater Son—God says:

> Also I will make him My *first-*
> *born,*
> The *highest of the kings* of the
>   earth (Psalm 89:27; emphasis
>   added).

Likewise, the angel Gabriel proclaimed to Mary:

> He will be great, and will be called the Son of the Highest;
> and the Lord God *will give Him* the throne of His father
> David. And He will reign over the house of Jacob forever,
> and of His kingdom there will be no end (Luke 1:32-33;
> emphasis added).

And to this "Son of the Highest" God also said:

> Ask of Me, and I will give You
>   The nations for Your *inheritance,*
> And the ends of the earth for
>   Your *possession* (Psalm 2:8; emphasis added).

The Son is the Heir *par excellence!* As God's firstborn in status
(His Sonship is eternal) His future inheritance is the entire world,
which He will rule from the throne of His father David. God has
appointed Him "heir of all things" (Heb. 1:2)!

Can Christians enter into *this* inheritance? Can they become
joint-heirs (see Rom. 8:17b) with the King?[3] It is obvious that
they can.

But it is also obvious that this is a *meritorious* heirship, and not
one conferred by grace alone:

> If we endure,
>   We shall also reign with Him (2 Tim. 2:12).

The Scriptures bear powerful and repeated testimony to this
truth. As we have seen already, the productive servants in our
Lord's parable of the minas received ten and five cities respec-
tively. The unproductive servant received none.

Similarly in the letters to the seven churches, the risen Christ
conditions the sharing of His royal power on obedience and
victorious living. So we read:

> And he who overcomes, and keeps My works until the
> end, to him I will give power over the nations—"He shall

> rule them with a rod of iron; they shall be dashed to
> pieces like the potter's vessels"—(Rev. 2:26-27).

And again:

> To him who overcomes I will grant to sit with Me on My
> throne, as I also overcame and sat down with My Father
> on His throne (Rev. 3:21).

Even in that grand scene which is described in the Book of
Revelation, after our Lord has triumphantly returned to reign,
we still encounter the theme of heirship. For there the rulers of
the world to come are described as having a "portion" in the first
resurrection. But the Greek word for "portion" can signify a
"share" in an inheritance, or the inheritance itself.[4]

It is, in fact, this very word which the Prodigal Son used when
he asked for his inheritance ahead of time:

> And the younger of them said to his father, "Father, give
> me the *portion* of goods that falls to me." So he divided
> to them his livelihood (Luke 15:12; emphasis added).

One should note also the prominence of the Old Testament word
for "portion," to signify an inheritance or a possession, as in the
passage quoted earlier:

> You shall have no *inheritance* in their land, nor shall you
> have any *portion* among them; I am your *portion* and your
> *inheritance* . . . . (Num. 18:20; emphasis added).

The words of the Apostle John, therefore, are rich with significance when he writes:

> And I saw thrones, and they sat on them, and judgment
> was committed to them. Then I saw the souls of those
> who had been beheaded for their witness to Jesus and
> for the word of God, who had not worshipped the beast
> or his image, and had not received his mark on their
> foreheads or on their hands. And they lived and reigned
> with Christ a thousand years (Rev. 20:4).

Here the theme of merit is unmistakable. The faithful martyrs of
the Great Tribulation are rewarded with a share in Christ's royal
power.

What the seer says next, however, has been widely misread. John's words are:

Blessed and holy is he who has *part* [a portion] in the first resurrection. Over such the second death has no power, but they shall be priests of God and of Christ, and shall reign with Him a thousand years (Rev. 20:6; emphasis added).

It would be wrong to read these words in a vacuum. The text *need not* be construed as saying that certain people simply "take part" in the first resurrection. On the contrary, John's vivid statements must be read against the background of our Lord's parable of the minas and against the background of all the other Scriptures already noted.

What we have here is co-heirship with Christ. In this splendid sphere of existence which is called "the first resurrection," there are those especially blessed because they have "a portion," "an inheritance," there. And that "inheritance" or "portion" is described as an immortality which entails priestly and kingly duties.

So these are the servants whose minas have multiplied into vibrant opportunities for further activity for their Lord. They are, in short, the joint-heirs of God's firstborn Son, and this is their "portion"—this is their role—in the world to come.

Kingly Character

Since the superlative privilege of reigning with Christ is contingent on our faithfulness to Him, it follows that the joint-heirs are people whose personalities have been molded by a spirit of obedience. It is not surprising, therefore, that the Scripture lays down character qualifications for those who aspire to possess a royal role in the Kingdom of God.

Thus, as Jesus opened the Sermon on the Mount with instructions for His disciples (Matt. 5:1-2), He said:

Blessed are the poor in spirit, for theirs is the kingdom of heaven (Matt. 5:3).

One beatitude later He declares:

> Blessed are the meek, for they shall inherit the earth
> (Matt. 5:5).

And He concludes this segment of His message with the words:

> Blessed are those who are persecuted for righteousness'
> sake, for theirs is the kingdom of heaven (Matt. 5:10).

The Kingdom, says Jesus, *belongs to* disciples whose lowly and submissive spirits seem impoverished in a world of arrogance and pride. It *belongs to* His followers who are persecuted because of their righteous lives. And the earth will someday be the property—the inheritance—of the meek![5]

There is no hint in such words that the Kingdom *belongs to* men as a gift of divine grace. Eternal life belongs to men that way—but not the Kingdom!

The heir of the Kingdom, then, must reflect the spirit of His Lord. His deeds and actions must be congruent with the standards of his Master. When this is not so, heirship is forfeited. The writer of Hebrews made this plain when he warned his readers to take care

> . . . lest there be any fornicator or profane person like
> Esau, who for one morsel of food sold his birthright (Heb.
> 12:16).

The Greek expression rendered "birthright" here signifies Esau's special inheritance rights as Isaac's firstborn son. Being a man of low moral standards and little spirituality, he was willing to part with his rights for a temporary, physical gratification. "Beware," the author means, "that none of you do likewise."[6]

In a similar fashion, the Apostle Paul cautioned his Christian brethren against the forfeiture of heirship through immoral living. He wrote pointedly about this to the Corinthians:

> Do you not know that the unrighteous *will not inherit* the
> kingdom of God? Do not be deceived. Neither fornicators,
> nor idolaters, nor adulterers, nor homosexuals, nor sod-
> omites, nor thieves, nor covetous, nor drunkards, nor
> revilers, nor extortioners *will inherit* the kingdom of God.
> And such were some of you. But you were washed, but
> you were sanctified, but you were justified in the name of

the Lord Jesus and by the Spirit of our God (1 Cor. 6:9-
11; emphasis added; see also Gal. 5:19-21; Eph. 5:5-6).

It is unfortunate that these words have been so widely miscon-
strued. When the thought of "inheriting" the Kingdom is
reduced to a mere synonym for "entering" it, the force of the
warning is largely lost.

The unsavory descriptions in Paul's list of vices had fit many
of the Corinthians in their unsaved days. But God had mercifully
washed their past away as He sanctified and justified them by
His saving grace. Their past, therefore, no longer stood as a
barrier to heirship in God's Kingdom.

But the present could, and this is Paul's point. "The unright-
eous will not inherit the kingdom of God," he insists, and he has
just charged them with behaving unrighteously:

No, you yourselves *do wrong* [Greek = act unrighteously]
and cheat, and you do these things to your brethren! (1
Cor. 6:8; emphasis added).

But not only that, there was a case of incest in the Corinthian
church (5:1) and the apostle will shortly urge them to "flee
immorality" (6:18; see vv. 12-20). Their present conduct, then,
imperiled their heirship.

This does not mean, of course, that if a believer commits one
of these sins he is forever barred from reigning with Christ.
Should he fall, God's cleansing and restoring grace can be his
again (1 John 1:9) and he can cease to be a person like that.

But suppose Christ comes and finds me walking in unjudged
sins of this kind? Suppose I am, at His coming, an adulterer or a
thief or a drunkard or any of the other things mentioned here?
In that case, the Scripture is plain. I am the kind of person who
cannot inherit the Kingdom of God! But these spiritual conditions, as deplorable as they are, do not jeopardize the Christian's
"entrance" into God's Kingdom. That remains a gift of God's
matchless grace.

Be Ready!

No wonder then that the Scriptures lay such stress on how Christ finds us when He comes back. We have already listened to John's words:

> And now, little children, abide in Him, that when He appears, we may have confidence and not be ashamed before Him at His coming (1 John 2:28).

And Peter also admonishes us:

> Therefore, beloved, looking forward to these things, be diligent *to be found by Him* in peace, without spot and blameless (2 Pet. 3:14; emphasis added).

But the most solemn warning of all was issued by the King Himself.

On one occasion the Lord Jesus had spoken at length concerning the events surrounding His second advent. In the midst of this great exposition of future things—we call it the Olivet Discourse—the Son of God had inserted a parable designed to warn and challenge His servants.

He began the parable this way:

> Who then is a faithful and wise servant, whom his master made ruler over his household, to give them food in due season? Blessed is that servant whom his master, *when he comes*, will find so doing. Assuredly, I say to you that he will make him ruler over all his goods (Matt. 24:45-47; emphasis added).

Here again is co-heirship with the coming King. The servant who is faithfully performing his duties, *when his Master arrives*, is elevated to a position with sweeping authority: "He will make him ruler over all his goods."

But another outcome for this servant's career looms as a somber possibility:

> But if that evil servant says in his heart, "My master is delaying his coming," and begins to beat his fellow servants, and to eat and drink with the drunkards, the master of that servant *will come on a day when he is not*

looking for him, and at an hour that he is not aware of,
and will cut him in two and appoint him his *portion* with
the hypocrites. There shall be weeping and gnashing of
teeth (Matt. 24:48-51; emphasis added).

Naturally, we must not suppose, as many have done, that our
Lord speaks here of an unsaved man. He is still talking about the
same individual whom he has just described as a potential ruler
over His goods. The words, "But if *that* evil servant . . . ," make
this plain.

Morever, this wicked slave is *not* an unbeliever at all. He
actually believes in the coming of his Lord but has persuaded
himself that this coming will be postponed: "My master is delay-
ing his coming"! But this was his fatal error. No longer moved by
a sense of watchfulness, his lifestyle degenerates rapidly. He
begins to mistreat his Christian brethren (his "fellow servants")
and then to indulge himself with intemperate and base behavior.
He eats and drinks with the drunkards.[7]

In this lamentable state of soul, the servant is utterly unprepared for his Master's arrival and for the day of accounting that
follows. Indeed, his Judge cuts him to pieces!

Of course, Jesus was dealing here in metaphor. The English
rendering ("cut him in two") is too precise. The underlying
Greek verb can signify "to cut something up," and it should be
evident that this expression is a figure of speech. Not even
unsaved people will ever be *literally* cut to pieces! How much
less Jesus' own servants!

But the day of accounting is nonetheless dreadful for the
unfaithful servant of Christ. The "terror of the Lord" will be, for
such a man, only too real. And the instrument by which his
failed life will be judged is sharp indeed:

For the word of God is living and powerful, and sharper
than any two-edged sword, piercing even to the division
of soul and spirit, and of joints and marrow, and is a
discerner of the thoughts and intents of the heart. And
there is no creature hidden from His sight, but all things

> are naked and open to the eyes of Him *to whom we must give an account* (Heb. 4:12-13; emphasis added).

No doubt, for the kind of man whom our Lord's parable describes, the Judgment Seat of Christ will seem like an exquisitely painful surgery on his soul. The sharp, two-edged sword of the divine Word will "bring to light the hidden things of darkness and reveal the counsels of the heart" (1 Cor. 4:5). Surely the agony of exposure will be indescribably acute.[8]

But in addition to that, there is no co-heirship with Christ. Instead—and the irony is powerful—there *is* co-heirship with hypocrites! For He will "appoint him his *portion* with the hypocrites. There shall be weeping and gnashing of teeth."

This servant had become a hypocrite. *Not* a hypocrite in the sense that he only pretended to be a Christian. Such a thought is totally extraneous to this text. Instead, he had occupied the position and role of a servant of Christ, and had ended by serving only himself. His role was ostensibly to feed his Lord's household, but instead he beat his fellow-servants and indulgently fed himself. And that was hypocrisy! Profound regret was its rightful legacy.[9]

Tragically, there is no reason to think that there will not be many such hypocrites standing at the Judgment Seat of Christ. Like the fearful servant in the parable of the minas they will hear their Lord's stinging rebuke, and it will be as though a two-edged sword pierced their innermost being. They will experience deep shame. They will weep and gnash their teeth.

Not forever, of course. Indeed, perhaps only for a short time. For ultimately God will wipe away every tear from their eyes (Rev. 21:4). But those who cannot conceive of a Christian grieving deeply over an unfaithful life, and sorrowing profoundly over a lost heirship, are not being realistic. In fact, it is precisely the glorified saint, free at last from the deluding influences of sin, who will likely be most moved with unutterable sadness over a life that has been poorly invested for God.

To Receive a Kingdom

The nobleman in the Savior's parable went into a far country "to receive for himself a kingdom and to return" (Luke 19:12, see v. 15). The language of His words was easily recognized as a reference to the acquisition of kingly authority. It is noteworthy that very similar words were used in this sense in the Greek translation of the Old Testament writings.[10]

But while the nobleman was away, His servants served Him. As they did so, they too were "receiving a kingdom." Their service constituted them "partners" with the coming King, and "co-heirs" with God's firstborn Son. But their service needed to go on right to the very end. Should they turn from this at any time, there was the danger that they would be overtaken suddenly by their Master's return.

This would be a calamity of unspeakable magnitude. They needed, therefore, to cling to God's strength and rely on His grace, to keep on serving Him well. They needed to be aware of God's awesome holiness which, like an all-devouring flame, could reduce man's pretensions and hypocrisy to ashes. They needed to understand that they must someday meet their God in the Person of His Son and, with Him as their Judge, submit their lives to the fiery trial of His all-knowing gaze (cf. 1 Cor. 3:11-15).

It is understandable, therefore, that at the climax of his powerful Epistle, the author of Hebrews writes:

> Therefore, since we are *receiving a kingdom* which cannot be shaken, let us have grace, by which we may *serve God* acceptably with reverence and godly fear. For our God is a consuming fire (Heb. 12:28-29; emphasis added).[11]

CHAPTER

9

THE DARKNESS OUTSIDE

A time of great joy awaits the Heir of all things. For the present, He has gone into the "far country" of heaven to receive His Kingdom. At God's appointed time He will return to reign and to rejoice.

The anticipation of this joy to come is nowhere more beautifully expressed than in the words of the writer of Hebrews, as he urges his readers to consider the Lord Jesus Christ:

> ... the author and finisher of our faith, who *for the joy that was set before Him* endured the cross, despising the shame, and has sat down at the right hand of the throne of God (Heb. 12:2; emphasis added).

We are not left to imagine what kind of joy the inspired author has in mind, since he has spoken of it plainly in the opening chapter of this epistle. There, quoting the ancient psalmist, he writes of God's Son:

> Your throne, O God, is forever and ever;
> A scepter of righteousness is the scepter of Your
>   Kingdom.

You have loved righteousness and hated lawlessness;
Therefore God, Your God, has anointed You
With the oil of gladness more than your companions.
(Heb. 1:8-9, quoting Psalm 45:6-7; emphasis added.)

As the larger context of the psalm discloses, the first half of it (vv. 1-9) describes the King fully trimphant over His enemies, whose throne is eternally established, and whose kingly joy is shared by His "companions."

The final half of the psalm (vv. 10-17) describes a beautiful, regal woman to whom the King is evidently to be married. She is accompanied by virgins, her own companions (v. 14), and she is challenged to forget her paternal home as she becomes the wife of the King (vv. 10-11). Thus the psalm as a whole presents the splendor and festivity of a royal wedding.[1]

In this lovely poem, the psalmist no doubt foresees that future day of surpassing joy, when Messiah's eternal Kingdom is established on earth, and when He is thereby permanently "married" to His own city, land, and nation. The theme of wedding joy, whether for Israel, the land itself, or Mt. Zion and Jerusalem, runs prominently throughout Old Testament prophecy. It finds articulation again and again.

Among the many beautiful expressions of this theme are the words of Hosea, who wrote:

"And it shall be, in that day,"
Says the Lord,
"That you will call Me 'My Husband,'
And no longer call Me 'My Master' " . . . .
"I will betroth you to Me forever;
Yes, I will betroth you to Me
In righteousness and justice,
In loving kindness and mercy;
I will betroth you to Me in faithfulness,
And you shall know the Lord."
(Hosea 2:16, 19-20.)

Or, again, Isaiah proclaims:

For Zion's sake I will not hold My peace,

And for Jerusalem's sake I will not rest,
Until her righteousness goes forth as brightness,
And her salvation as a lamp that burns . . . .
You shall also be a crown of glory
In the hand of the Lord,
And a royal diadem
In the hand of your God.
You shall no longer be termed Forsaken,
Nor your land any more be termed Desolate;
But you shall be called Hephzibah [= My Delight in Her]
    and your land Beulah [= Married];
For the Lord delights in you,
And your land shall be married.
For as a young man marries a virgin,
So shall your sons marry you;
And as the bridegroom rejoices over the bride,
So shall your God rejoice over you.
(Isa. 62:1, 3-5.)

Naturally, it was to be expected that so exquisite a simile, or metaphor, should find a significant place in the teachings of Jesus Himself. After all, He *personally* was the King whose special joy in that day would exceed the joy of all others. But He would also have companions to share this joy with Him (Heb. 1:9). And these companions must understand on what terms they could enter into the joy of their Lord, and what demands this privilege placed upon them right here and now.

To attain that joy, the King Himself had endured the cross and despised the shame (Heb. 12:2). He now sat at the right hand of the throne of God awaiting the very subjugation of His enemies which the psalmist had so graphically portrayed (Heb. 12:2; 10:12-13; Psalm 43:3-5). It was precisely because He had loved righteousness and hated wickedness that His God had anointed Him with the oil of gladness more than His companions (Ps. 45:7).

That was *His* reward! It would be no different for His companions. For although they could not love righteousness as perfectly as He did, nor hate wickedness as completely as He did, they could nevertheless follow His example and share His joy to a significant degree.

And that was co-heirship. It was to share royal dignity and prerogatives—and royal joy!—with the King. So bright and luminous was such a prospect, that to be excluded from this experience might well be described as a kind of banishment into darkness, where such shining happinesses were beyond one's capacity to attain, or even to comprehend.

To put it another way, to be excluded from this honor was like being expelled from a royal wedding celebration.

The Man with No Wedding Garment

To make this truth vivid and real to men, Jesus once told a parable about a man who accepted a wedding invitation, but failed to come properly dressed for the occasion and was ignominiously put out into the dark. The parable has caused significant perplexity among Christian readers, mainly because its parabolic nature has not been kept clearly in mind.

Then, too, the problem has been compounded by the fact that in much of the evangelical world God's rich grace has suffered significant eclipse. Parables such as this one are not read with the simplicity that a firm grasp of the Christian gospel ought to make possible. This multiplies the likelihood that their real message will go unheard.

The opening statement of the Savior's parable announces that "the kingdom of heaven is like a certain king who arranged a marriage for his son" (Matt. 22:2). The invitations are then sent out and are refused. This is followed by a fresh round of invitations which are likewise spurned, but also the king's servants are mistreated and killed (22:3-6). The king then sends out his armies, kills these murderers, and burns up their city (22:7).

How skillfully does our Lord paint the sad history of the Jewish rejection of God's purposes! The Kingdom He Himself

preached to them (Matt. 4:17) they were in the process of refusing, and their city, Jerusalem, was destined to be burned to the
ground by the Roman armies, which God used as His instrument
of judgment.

But the rich and special joys of the wedding celebration were
not to be abandoned just because some had spurned them. The
king's son must have companions! So the servants of the king are
now sent on a wider circuit which this time included the highways beyond the city, and they are urged to invite all whom they
found (22:8-9). This they do, and without regard to character or
attainment, so that we read:

> So those servants went out into the highways and gath-
> ered together all whom they found, both bad and good.
> And the wedding hall was filled with guests (Matt. 22:10).

Of course, as our Lord had pointed out to the rich young ruler,
in the full sense of the word, "no one is good but One, that is
God" (Mark 10:18). Nevertheless, from a human point of view,
Paul could speak of a "good man" (Rom. 5:7), and the two
named converts of the Evangelist Philip—Simon Magus and the
Ethiopian eunuch (Acts 8:9-40)—were opposites of the kind suggested in this parable. One was steeped in sorcery, the other was
steeped in Scripture. But both, on scriptural testimony, became
Christians (8:13, 38). The "bad" and the "good" were gathered
in.

In like manner, the invitation to experience the special joys of
the Kingdom of God—the call to co-heirship with Jesus Christ—
is not confined to those with the special qualities which men find
attractive and admirable. Instead, it is an invitation that has
already overleaped the barriers of Judaism and proceeds along
the highways of larger humanity, seeking only hearers that are
willing to come, whether they be "bad" or "good."

But it is to the wedding supper itself, and not merely to the
Kingdom as such, that the call is extended. That certainly implies
a saving belief in the message about the King's Son. But it
involves more than that. It involves also a willingness to be His

disciple, to love righteousness and hate wickedness as He did, to take up our own cross as He took up His.

In short, it involves a willingness to enter the Kingdom prepared for its special privileges. It means coming to the wedding properly dressed!

What follows in the parable no doubt reaches its central point:

> But when the king came in to see [or, observe] the guests, he saw a man there who did not have on a wedding garment. So he said to him, "Friend, how did you come in here without a wedding garment?" And he was speechless (Matt. 22:11-12).

Naturally, some have thought that the garment lacked by the man in question was a "robe of righteousness" which the king would have given him freely. But the parable itself does not suggest this. Indeed, it seems not to have been the custom in those days.[2] The invitation to attend was freely given, but the one who accepted the call took it upon himself to obtain and wear suitable attire.

This man, then, had failed to carry out an obligation which his acceptance of the King's invitation placed upon him. It is surely not hard for the Christian reader to detect in the appearance of the king, who then "observes" the assembled guests, another clear reference to the day of accounting which lies ahead for every Christian. In that day our garments—our life and its works—will come under God's scrutiny and evaluation.

To be sure, we have also accepted an invitation to *live* in God's Kingdom. That destiny can be ours by simple faith alone, and is never subject at all to divine review. But to set foot on the pathway of Christian living is to hear God's call to the highest privileges which eternity affords. It is to respond to the challenge to become joint-heirs with the King and to enter richly into His special joys. But before the celebration begins, there must come the review!

The next words are solemn:

> Then the king said to the servants, "Bind him hand and foot, take him away, and cast him into outer darkness;

there will be weeping and gnashing of teeth." For many
are called, but few are chosen (Matt. 22:13-14).

Solemn, yes! But not so grim as they are usually made out to be.

Most Christian readers identify the "outer darkness" as a
description of hell.[3] They would be surprised to learn that the
Greek phrase employed here is used only three times, all in
Matthew (8:12; 22:13; 25:30), and nowhere else in the New Testament. It is true that Peter and Jude describe hell in terms of
abysmal darkness (2 Pet. 2:4, 17; Jude 13), but Matthew's words
take a form distinctive to his Gospel. They might be idiomati-
cally rendered "the darkness outside."[4]

Here one must keep firmly in mind that we are dealing with a
parable filled with symbolic elements. The man's hands and feet
are bound, our Lord reports. But no one takes this binding
literally, even if it is thought that an unsaved man is in view.
Indeed, the wedding garment he lacks is not literal, nor for that
matter is the wedding supper itself.

The Savior's parable is a magnificent metaphor. It visualizes
the kingly joys of God's Son under the familiar Old Testament
image of a wedding celebration. The invited guests are called to
participate in these joys, and their wedding garments are sym-
bols of their successful efforts to prepare themselves for these.
But the man who lacked the garment was unprepared for such
special privileges. His activities in the Kingdom of God thus
come under severe restrictions as his hands and feet are bound.
Like the servant who hid the mina (Luke 14:26), the man is not
allowed to be *active* for his Lord in the experience of joint
heirship. The "darkness outside" is a powerful, evocative image
for the exclusion he experiences as a result.

There is no suggestion here of punishment or torment. The
presence of remorse, in the form of weeping and gnashing of
teeth, does not in any way require this inference.[5] Indeed, what
we actually see in the image itself is a man soundly "trussed up"
out on the darkened grounds of the king's private estate, while
the banquet hall glows with light and reverberates with the joys
of those inside.[6] That is what we actually see. *And that is all!*

But that is enough! We do not need to embellish the parable with the lurid colors of eternal damnation. There is no fire and brimstone on the king's handsome estate, no worms of corruption creeping out from under the boulders of his well-kept grounds. This is what has been read into the story. But it isn't there. A parable, after all, has its natural limits and these we must be careful not to breach.

We are not to deduce, either, that the failing Christian will spend an anguished eternity in some darkened corner of God's Kingdom with nothing meaningful at all to do. That, too, would be a grotesque distortion of our Lord's teaching.

No, it is enough to say that the failing Christian has missed a splendid experience of co-reigning with Christ, with all the multiplied joys which that experience implies. It is enough to affirm that he undergoes a significant exclusion from the "light and gladness, joy and honor" (see Esther 8:16) which the co-heirs experience with Christ. Whatever else eternity holds for him, he has at least missed *that!*

If he can view such a loss with equanimity now, our Lord makes it clear that he will not view it that way hereafter: "There will be weeping and gnashing of teeth."

And well there might be! The unfaithful Christian, like the ill-dressed guest, has missed the wedding supper just as surely as did those who spurned the invitation to begin with. Thus he joins the crowded ranks of the many who are called to co-heirship, and misses the elite number of the few who actually attain it.

And that is certainly worth crying about!

The Unprofitable Servant

The rude guest who came to the wedding improperly attired is but another of our Lord's effective portraits of a failing servant of God. In him we glimpse again the servant who hid his mina (Luke 19:20-16), or the one who concluded that his Lord's coming was delayed and who slipped into a belligerent and self-indulgent style of living (Matt. 24:48-51).

Thus we are not surprised when such a man emerges in a parable strikingly similar to the one about the minas. The story is found near the end of the Savior's great exposition of prophetic truth, called the Olivet Discourse. It is traditionally known as the parable of the talents (Matt. 25:14-30).

Here, as before, we encounter the Master's trip into a far country and a commitment of money into the hands of the servants who are left behind (Matt. 14:14). The talent, however, was a substantially larger amount of money than the mina, and was a unit of monetary reckoning whose value was always high. Unlike the previous parable, the servants are not viewed as equal, but as charged with responsibilities appropriate to their ability to carry them out (25:15). This, of course, is simply another side of Christian accountability. The day of assessment will evaluate our performance in terms of the God-given capacity to perform. We will be measured in terms of our own abilities, not in terms of the abilities of others.

The servant in the parable who had the maximum ability—and hence, the maximum responsibility (ten talents)—performs well in his Lord's absence. He multiplies his Lord's investment 100 percent, gaining ten more talents, and is suitably rewarded:

Well done, good and faithful servant; you were faithful over a few things. I will make you *ruler over many things.* Enter into *the joy of your lord* (Matt. 25:21; emphasis added).

It seems plain that co-heirship with the King is once again in view. This faithful man, despite what by common standards seemed a huge amount of money, is told that until now he has actually been the guardian of only a small sum: a "few things." His new position, by comparison, dwarfs his previous responsibility: "I will make you RULER over *many*" things! This pronouncement is followed at once by an invitation to *enter into* the King's personal joy!

It is an encouraging feature of this form of our Savior's parable that the second servant, though less competent than the previous one (he has received only five talents), has nevertheless maximized his own opportunities as well. He is able to give his Master also a 100 percent return—five additional talents. His commendation and reward are *identical* with those of his more capable brother (25:23). He, too, becomes a joint-heir with access to his Lord's joy at precisely the same level as the ten-talent man.

Obviously, such could have been the experience of the servant with one talent as well if he had but gained a mere additional talent. But he had not. And with words fully reminiscent of the reasonings of the servant who wrapped his mina in a handkerchief, this sad failure of a man digs up the buried money and returns it to his Lord.

The King's response to him stands in total contrast to His response to the faithful servants. Whereas they had received His warm *commendation* ("Well done, good and faithful servant"), this man receives His ringing *condemnation*:

> You wicked and lazy servant, you knew that I reap where
> I have not sown, and gather where I have not scattered
> seed. Therefore you ought to have deposited my money
> with the bankers, and at my coming I would have received
> back my own with interest" (Matt. 25:26-27).

There is certainly nothing here to suggest an unbeliever. This was a man with real responsibility given to him by his Master, and the fundamental charge is that he had not acted on the knowledge of his Master's character which he himself admitted that he had. That the Judgment Seat of Christ is before us in this scene is an observation that ought not to require making.

It follows that the failing servant is denied the opportunity to rule—not merely only over many things, but over anything at all! Whereas *promotion* to additional responsibility had come to the previous servants, *demotion* from responsibility comes to him:

> Therefore take the talent from him, and give it to him who
> has ten talents. For to everyone who has, more will be
> given, and he will have abundance; but from him who
> does not have, even what he has will be taken away
> (Matt. 25:28-29).

Once more there is the tragedy of deprivation. Once more there are the bound hands and feet.

And once more there is "the darkness outside":

And cast the unprofitable servant into the outer darkness. There will be weeping and gnashing of teeth (Matt. 25:30).

At this point, of course, most readers lose touch with the obvious overall thrust of the parable and think at once of hell. But it *is* after all a parable! There are no literal sums of money— whether twenty talents, ten, or one—to be laid down at the feet of the Judge, either at the Judgment Seat of Christ or at the Great White Throne. Instead, as in the parable previously considered, we are in the presence of metaphor.

"The darkness outside" is the reverse of "the joy inside." The faithful servants *enter into* the joy of their Lord. The unfaithful servant is *excluded from* that joy. The image of the wedding celebration (Matt. 22) hovers in the background of the reader's mind and permits him to interpret the imagery properly.

The judgment of the two kinds of servants is thus skillfully contrasted. The faithful servants experience *commendation, promotion*, and *access to joy*. The unfaithful servant experiences *condemnation, demotion*, and *exclusion from joy*. The former reign joyfully with the King. The latter does not.

The Supreme Reward

No doubt eternity holds many special joys and many special rewards for the people of God. Even a cup of cold water given in the name of a disciple "shall by no means lose" its due reward (Matt. 10:41-42). God never forgets anything that has been truly done for Him (Heb. 6:10).

But the stress which the recorded teaching of Jesus lays upon the privilege of ruling with Him makes it plain that this is the highest reward of all. And for this, much more is required than an occasional good deed here and there.

Certainly, when the Apostle Paul describes for us the fire that will test our life's work, his image is well-chosen for its impressive flexibility. Thus he can write:

For no other foundation can anyone lay than that which is laid, which is Jesus Christ. Now if anyone builds on this foundation with gold, silver, precious stones, wood, hay, straw, each one's work will become manifest; for the Day will declare it, because it will be revealed by fire; and the fire will test each one's work, of what sort it is. If anyone's work which he has built on it endures, he will receive a reward. If anyone's work is burned, he will suffer loss; but he himself will be saved, yet so as through fire (1 Cor. 3:11-15).

The value of this apostolic instruction can hardly be praised too much. Suppose a man's works are utterly burned up, is his salvation threatened because of that? No! says Paul. "He himself will be saved"! But the fiery ordeal of the Judgment Seat of Christ, through which he must pass, will not easily be forgotten.

But Paul's metaphor also permits us to visualize a man who builds largely with wood, hay, and straw, yet manages a pearl or a diamond here and there. The conflagration on the day of reckoning will be considerable, but there will also be something left to reward. And God, we may be certain, will do so with the generosity which is so much a part of His nature.

But a life largely constructed of perishable materials is obviously not what our Lord requires of His co-heirs. In such servants the Savior seeks an accounting in which His investment in them reaps a profit. This is evident particularly from the parables about the minas and the talents. Hence, a life "saved," rather than a life left in ruins, is what He demands of those who would enter into His royal authority and joy.

And those believers who fail to attain to that kind of experience are like runners in a race who are disqualified for the crown. Such was the possibility that even Paul confronted seriously and sought earnestly to avoid (1 Cor. 9:24-27).[7]

But if it was a race, obviously staying power was part of the process. It was necessary to reach the finish line, for only there was the crown of victory dispensed. Hence, amid the hardships and fatigue which the contest entailed, one needed always to keep this truth in mind: "If we *endure*, we shall also reign with Him" (2 Tim. 2:12). Or, as the Son of God Himself had put it so effectively:

> And he who overcomes, and *keeps My works until the end*, to him I will give power over the nations—
> "He shall rule them with a rod of iron;
> They shall be dashed to pieces like the potter's vessels"—
> *as I also have received from My Father.*
> (Rev. 2:26-27; emphasis added.)

So these were to be the joint-heirs. They were the servants of Christ who endured to the end and shared the kingly prerogatives the Father had given to His Son. They were the King's companions in unspeakable, eternal joy (Heb. 1:9).

What a brilliant and glorious prospect! Here was a bright anticipation that offered the fulfillment of man's deepest aspirations. Indeed, through that unique mastery of words which the Lord Jesus so clearly possessed, this truth became a hope which shone before His followers like a distant banquet hall gleaming with light and echoing with the joy of a wondrous wedding celebration.

And once that scene has been truly glimpsed, who would want to be left in "the darkness outside"?

CHAPTER

10

THE OVERCOMERS

No earthly banquet was ever so splendid. No roster of assembled guests was ever so impressive. The co-heirs of King Jesus are the elite of human history. To be numbered among them is the highest honor—and greatest victory!—which any man or woman can achieve.[1]

But what is it that really makes an overcomer? What are the secrets of his victorious life? Some of these secrets have already come before us in the various Scriptures pertaining to this theme. But some deserve special stress from passages which have not yet been considered.

Spiritual victory is not an accident. It is, after all, the outworking of the fundamental truths and principles which permeate the Word of God. The would-be overcomer needs to grasp these principles firmly. He needs to live these truths out in daily life.

Abundant Faith

Without exception, the overcomer is a man or a woman of great faith.

It was apparently not long after completing his famous Sermon on the Mount (Matt. 5-7) that Jesus encountered a Gentile with remarkable faith (Matt. 8:5-13). He was a Roman centurion whose servant was desperately sick. But so great was this man's confidence in the word of Jesus that he was able to say to Him:

> Lord, I am not worthy that You should come under my roof. But only speak a word and my servant will be healed. For I also am a man under authority, having soldiers under me. And I say to this one, "Go," and he goes; and to another, "Come," and he comes; and to my servant, "Do this," and he does it (Matt. 8:8-9).

Clearly, here was a man with supreme confidence in the *authority* of the word of Jesus. But it was precisely this note of authority that had astonished His audience on the Mount (Matt. 7:28-29). Nevertheless, one could not effectively build his life (his "house") on Jesus' words (see Matt. 7:24-27) unless he had confidence like that of the centurion in Jesus' authority.

No wonder, then, that the centurion's words elicit from Jesus not only high praise but His very first recorded reference to the banquet of co-heirship:

> When Jesus heard it, He marveled, and said to those who followed, "Assuredly, I say to you, I have not found such great faith, not even in Israel! And I say to you that many will come from east and west, and sit down [recline] with Abraham, Isaac, and Jacob in the kingdom of heaven. But the sons of the kingdom will be cast into outer darkness [the darkness outside]. There will be weeping and gnashing of teeth" (Matt. 8:10-12).

It is unmistakable that our Lord's great metaphor about the wedding supper shimmers in the background of these words. The imagery will later be developed more fully by the master Teacher of men, but it is here already in embryonic form.

Abraham, Isaac, and Jacob, we are told, are *reclining* in the Kingdom of heaven. The word used for this was quite commonly employed to describe someone reclining at a table to eat food. One begins, therefore, to visualize some great chamber or room in which these Old Testament worthies are assembled to dine with many others from the east and west. Since great banquets were normally held in the ancient Middle East at night, by inference one can conceive of "the darkness outside" as the region just beyond the brightly lighted hall where the festivities take place.

To be sure, this incipient image will be greatly sharpened by the Savior's future instruction, but its general outlines are present already. And one thing is clear: The guest list is impressive. It includes the three patriarchs of the Jewish race, who in their own right were men of great faith (see Heb. 11:8-16). And it includes Gentiles—like this centurion—who will come from the far corners of the earth to celebrate with the illustrious heroes of days gone by.

But almost equally impressive is the roster of the excluded: "But the sons of the kingdom will be cast into the darkness outside"!

The "sons of the Kingdom"? What a surprise! Yet in quoting this expression from the lips of Jesus, Matthew employs a phrase which (like "the darkness outside") is found only in his Gospel. Indeed, its only other occurrence in the entire New Testament is in the Savior's interpretation of the wheat and the tares, as reported in Matthew 13:36-43. "The good seed"—the wheat— "are the sons of the kingdom," said Jesus, "but the tares are the sons of the wicked one" (13:38).

So it was not that "the sons of the kingdom" did not belong in the *Kingdom*. They *did* belong there, as the tares did not. But they did not belong at the same *banquet* as Abraham, Isaac, and Jacob unless—like the centurion—they were people of great faith.

These words, of course, were directed at Jews. It was not that Jesus had not found *faith* in Israel. He had found it there. But

He had not found *"such great faith"* in Israel. He had not found faith like that which He had just now encountered in this centurion.

The crowds on the Mount who had listened to Jesus' Sermon *"were astonished"* at His authority (7:28). The centurion *believed* it!

Yes, faith got a man into God's Kingdom and made him a son of that Kingdom. But *great* faith could get him into the banquet! And there were Jewish sons of the Kingdom who would miss that banquet (while Gentiles from many quarters were admitted) unless their faith could be stretched beyond its present restricted limits. Precisely for this reason, the Roman centurion was a striking challenge to all to trust Christ's word completely and to construct one's life on the bedrock of His unshakable authority.

Great faith was thus often found in unlikely persons, like this Gentile. And for that reason, it was often found also among the poor.

Indeed, it was James, the Lord's own natural half-brother, who was later to write:

> Listen, my beloved brethren: Has God not chosen the poor of this world to be *rich in faith* and *heirs of the kingdom* which He promised to those who love Him?
> (James 2:5; emphasis added.)

James' readers had been making a mistake. They had been honoring the rich and slighting the poor (2:1-4). What a miscalculation that was! More often than not it was the Christian of little means who had a wealth of faith and thus was destined to become a co-heir with Jesus Christ, a co-possessor of His Kingdom.

It was hard for a man who trusted in riches even to *enter* God's Kingdom (Mark 10:24). And that took only a simple act of faith. But what of the lofty demands which devoted discipleship made on the would-be heir? That required *much* faith! And material destitution was often fertile soil for that kind of faith. The man who must trust God for the next meal will soon find he can trust Him for everything else as well. But material well-being was often—though not always—hard, resistant ground in which faith, if it existed there at all, thrived poorly.

Not surprisingly, therefore, Jesus Himself said to disciples who knew the meaning of earthly poverty:

> Blessed are you poor, for yours is the kingdom of God (Luke 6:20).

If one must choose, then, it would be far better to have little material wealth and an abundance of faith in God. After all, God's Kingdom *belonged* to people like that. No doubt a rich Christian could attain to co-heirship, but—James' words imply—their numbers were few!

Devotion to Christ

But another trait also marked the heir of God's Kingdom. God had promised that Kingdom, said James, "to those who love Him" (James 4:5). And great faith in God flourished naturally in an atmosphere of love for God.

In fact, as Jesus Himself made clear, love for Him stood at the root of a life of obedience (John 14:21-24), which in turn is the life of faith (Gal. 2:20). Not surprisingly, therefore, it was to disciples who had proved their devotion to Him that Jesus said:

> But you are those who have continued with Me in My trials. And I bestow upon you a kingdom, just as My Father bestowed one upon Me, that you may eat and drink at My table in My Kingdom, and sit on thrones judging the twelve tribes of Israel (Luke 22:28-30).

Here was co-heirship, of course, but this time described in literal terms rather than in parable. The apostles had been loyal to Jesus during His earthly trials (all, that is, except unsaved Judas who may already have left the room). The reward for this fidelity was a kingdom in which they would have distinct spheres of royal authority.[2] They were to serve as the King's regents over the twelve tribes of Israel. So prestigious and honorable was such a role that, when the King sat down to eat in His royal palace at the head table, these men would be privileged to sit there with Him!

"You . . . have continued with Me," said Jesus, knowing full well that before the night was over they would all forsake Him and flee. But he foresaw also their restoration and future usefulness (see Luke 22:31-32). He had given them a splendid appointment, which their subsequent apostolic careers fully ratified and confirmed. These men really loved Him (John 21:15-19). And because they did, they endured. Hence, they shall also reign with Him.

Kindness to Christ's Brethren

But who can love the King, without also loving those who belong to the King? Thus, too, the future co-heirs are marked by their kindness to Christ's brethren, however costly or dangerous such kindness may be.

Nowhere is this more clearly seen than in the co-heirs who come before the King immediately after the trying days of the Great Tribulation. In a passage often referred to as the judgment of the sheep and the goats, we are told how the living Gentiles are gathered before the King's glorious throne and separated into two differing groups (Matt. 25:31-33).

The sheep, who stand at the King's right hand, are saluted as heirs of the Kingdom:

> Come, you blessed of My Father, *inherit the kingdom* prepared for you from the foundation of the world: for I was hungry and you gave Me food; I was thirsty and you gave Me drink; I was a stranger and you took Me in; I was naked and you clothed Me; I was sick and you visited Me; I was in prison and you came to Me (Matt. 25:34-36; emphasis added).

Once again, as in *all* the New Testament texts that deal with inheriting the Kingdom, the stress on merit and good works, or good character, is plain and unmistakable. The Kingdom is not inherited by faith alone, it is only entered that way.

The goats, however, are wicked people who have done none of the good things that the sheep have done. They are sent away into everlasting punishment (25:46). They are unsaved.

There is no middle ground in this exceptional scene. There are no failing servants of Christ. But the reason for that has been explained earlier in the Olivet Discourse. The Great Tribulation is a period of such unparalleled, globe-spanning catastrophe that it threatens the extinction of the entire human race. Accordingly, Jesus affirmed:

> And unless those days were shortened, no flesh *would be saved*; but for the elect's sake those days will be shortened (Matt. 24:22; emphasis added).

But, as if that were not enough, this stressful era will be a time when evil reigns supreme. The Beast and the False Prophet, who are energized by Satan himself, dominate the world politically and economically (Rev. 13:1-8). As a result, many believers will succumb to the pressures of worldwide lawlessness and *will not be saved* from the ravishing judgments of the Great Tribulation.[3] Their lives will be swept away with millions of others. Their "houses" will collapse!

Jesus tells us this when He says:

> And then many will be offended, will betray one another, and will hate one another. . . . And because lawlessness shall abound, *the love of many will grow cold. But he who endures to the end shall be saved* (Matt. 24:10-12; emphasis added; connect "saved" here with "saved" in v. 22).

The sheep are Gentile believers whose love did not "grow cold," despite the arctic spiritual temperatures all around them. They have been careful for the well-being of the King's brethren, who are perhaps chiefly the Jewish missionaries who will spread the gospel during those climactic days (cf. Rev. 12:17; 14:1-7; Matt. 24:14).[4] Hated and hunted by the Beast, forbidden to buy or sell without his mark, these traveling servants of God will be utterly dependent on the aid of courageous believers. The unsaved world, deluded by the prevailing Satanic deceptions, will want nothing to do with such men.

Some of these brethren unquestionably are martyred, but will be raised to reign with Christ (Rev. 20:4). Others, though perhaps surviving, will experience hunger, thirst, nakedness, sickness, or imprisonment. But the Gentile believers have ministered to them in situations like that, and in doing so (to their surprise) they have ministered directly to the King! For it was the King who confronted the world of that day through the preaching of these His brethren! It was therefore the King to whom men responded.

The co-heirs have passed the test. They have endured to the end, and their lives have been saved out of the wreckage of a ruined world (see again Matt. 24:12). But something more awaits them, for finally we read of them:

And these [the goats] will go away into everlasting punishment, but the righteous into eternal life (Matt. 25:46).

It must be remembered, as Paul declared, that "flesh and blood cannot inherit the kingdom of God; nor does corruption inherit incorruption" (1 Cor. 15:50). At the moment of their encounter with the King, the sheep are people of flesh and blood. Their physical lives have been saved, but to enter into their heirship they must also be transformed. Hence, as this scene concludes, they enter *eternal life.*

Of course, they *already had it* by faith in the King. What happens here, therefore, is that the heirs become immortal, possessors of resurrection life itself. No doubt the transformation will be instantaneous for them, as it will be for living Christians at the Rapture of the Church (1 Cor. 15:51-53; 1 Thess. 4:15-18), but the transformation is still essential. If they could not enter the resurrection state of everlasting incorruption, neither could they inherit the incorruptible Kingdom of God.

But they do inherit the Kingdom, and deservedly so. They have stood loyally with the servants of Christ during history's most trying times. Can any who aspire to heirship do less?

Watchfulness

If the great trilogy of Christian virtues is considered, all three are markedly prominent in the King's joint-heirs. *Faith* they possess richly, *love* they exercise vigorously toward Christ, toward His servants, and toward all (Gal. 6:10). But *hope* also is a watchword of their earthly lives.

In a remarkable discourse with His own disciples, which is recorded only by Luke (12:22-53), Jesus condenses into brief scope an impressive number of themes that are related to co-heirship with Himself. In public, He had just told the parable about the rich fool who laid up treasure for himself and was not rich toward God (Luke 12:16-21). It was then that He turned specifically to His disciples (12:22).

His disciples, Jesus warns, must be careful not to worry about their material needs. They must learn rather to trust God for these (12:22-30). Their first priority must be the Kingdom of God. Indeed they are to *seek* it (12:31).

Why? The answer is impressive:

Do not fear, little flock, for it is your Father's good pleasure *to give you the kingdom* (Luke 12:32).

Seek the Kingdom, says Jesus, because God wants to *give it to you*.[5] He wants you to be co-heirs!

But this truth has practical applications at the level of material life, for Jesus adds:

Sell what you have and give alms; provide yourselves money bags which do not grow old, a treasure in the heavens that does not fail, where no thief approaches nor moth destroys. For where your treasure is, there your heart will be also (Luke 12:33-34).

It was excellent advice. (It was *not* a legalistic demand, as Peter's words to Ananias sufficiently show: Acts 5:4.) The disciple who truly seeks to acquire the Kingdom must be preoccupied with heavenly, rather than earthly, treasure. He must so handle the transient things of this life, that they abundantly enrich the life to come. Such is the pathway of the joint-heirs.

There follows these challenging words a fresh parable of Jesus which, though similar to others, is in some ways remarkably unique. In it, He says:

Let your waist be girded, and your lamps burning; and you yourselves be like men who wait for their master,

> when he will return from the wedding [wedding banquet],
> that when he comes and knocks they may open to him
> immediately. Blessed are those servants whom the
> master, when he comes, will find watching. Assuredly, I
> say to you that he will gird himself and have them sit
> down [recline] to eat, and will come and serve them (Luke
> 12:35-37).

Perhaps none of the Savior's utterances about co-heirship are more deeply touching than this one. In this fresh articulation of that great theme, the wedding supper is viewed as *past*, and the Master as returning *from it!* This is significant and instructive.

In those parables in which Master and servants take part together in the wedding festivities, the stress falls obviously on the thought of their shared experiences. The King thus has *companions* who *enter into* His personal joy. This is a rich and important truth.

But the parable under consideration looks at things differently. The metaphor of the nuptial banquet is employed with that flexibility which is so useful in figures of speech. It is as though the King's joy has been realized. Now that it has, the time has come for His servants to rejoice as well.

The servants have been watchful for their Lord's return from the wedding. Girded for service, and keeping their lamps alight during the darkest hours of the night, they have listened eagerly and attentively for His arrival. They are ready to respond instantly to His knock.

This must be rewarded. So, in a lovely reversal of roles, the Master becomes a Servant to His servants. For now it is He who girds Himself and directs them to recline at a table to eat. (The word for "recline" is the same as the one in Matt. 8:11.) Then He personally serves their food, for this is *their* banquet. This is *their* time of joy!

Marvelous transformation! Through the skilled imagery of the Savior, the King's banquet has become the slaves' banquet! Their devotion to Him—their unremitting watchfulness—have brought them a splendid experience of personal fulfillment. All their personal hungers are now satisfied as their Lord graciously ministers like a waiter serving the very finest of foods.

Such, then, is the *hope* which undergirds the watchful anticipation of the co-heirs. During their time of waiting, the spirit of their service has been: "Lord, what can I do for You?" Hence the spirit of their reward will be: "What can I, your Lord, do for *you*?"

Let there be no mistake about it! Watchfulness is an indispensable key to the overcoming life which leads to co-heirship with the King. But watchfulness is always sustained by hope.

CONCLUSION

Naturally there are other passages that might well be considered in connection with the theme of spiritual victory and reward. One readily thinks, for example, of the splendid promises made to the overcomers in our Lord's letters to the seven churches of Asia (Rev. 2 and 3).

Although a detailed consideration of these promises lies outside the design of this book, a few words need to be said about them. Under the shadow cast by the eclipse of grace, the overcomers of Revelation 2 and 3 have often been thought to describe all those who attain final salvation from hell. Thus the promises are regarded as presenting the destiny of every saved individual.

This general view is commonly presented in one of two distinctly diverse ways: On the one hand are those who think that a true Christian can be eternally lost if he fails to achieve the status of an overcomer. On the other hand are those who teach that all who are truly saved to begin with will overcome.

When carefully considered, however, both views have one significant feature in common. Both insist that there is no final salvation from hell apart from good works. When, therefore, our Lord spoke of him "who overcomes, and keeps my works to the end . . . ," He must (in these views) have been speaking of *all* who would ultimately escape damnation. Accordingly, those who did not keep His works to the end would go to hell. How far this

conclusion is from the teaching of the New Testament as a whole
will hopefully be quite evident to the reader of this book.

It is true, of course, that the Apostle John affirms that
"whatever is born of God overcomes the world" and goes on to
say that "our faith" is "the victory that has overcome the world"
(1 John 5:4). Moreover, he adds:

> Who is he who overcomes the world, but he who believes
> that Jesus is the Son of God? (1 John 5:5).

But these statements are in no way synonymous with the statements of Revelation 2 and 3. They are not only found in wholly
different books, but also in contexts different from each other.
To appeal to the letter of First John to interpret the promises in
Revelation simply because similar expressions are used, is totally
illicit.

What the apostle clearly wishes to affirm in First John is that
the very act of believing in Christ is a singular—and permanent—victory over the unbelieving world around us. Moreover,
this victory is the reason why obedience to God's commands is
not a burden to the believer (v. 4; see Matt. 11:28-30). But this is
very different from saying that the Christian has no other battles
to fight or that victory in every spiritual conflict is assured.
When the text in First John is used to affirm thoughts like this, it
is clearly being misused.

Indeed, conflict confronts Christians in a multitude of shapes
and forms. In Revelation 2 and 3, the problems described in each
church have their own distinctive character and nature. The
victory won by the overcomer at Pergamos, for example, does
not take exactly the same form as that of the overcomer at
Thyatira. For that matter, no two Christian lives are exactly the
same in terms of their struggles or their triumphs. The Risen
Christ is Lord of each unique Christian assembly and of each
unique person within that assembly.

In all the diversity, therefore, which the conditions in the
seven churches of Asia reflect, there is manifest struggle and the
hope of victory through grace. But these letters do not present
victory as a *certainty*, but rather as an *aspiration* which each

individual should pursue. The Savior's words are never to *them* who overcome, but to *him* who overcomes. Victory is not a collective right, but an individual attainment.

Clearly, the promises to the overcomers are rewards for obedience to the commands of the Lord of the Church. As someone has pointedly observed, "A command that everyone keeps is superfluous, and a reward that everyone receives for a virtue that everyone has is nonsense."[6]

Two promises in particular have been thought to impinge on the eternal salvation of the overcomer. These are the ones made in the letters to Smyrna and Sardis. To those in Smyrna it is said:

He who overcomes shall not be hurt by the second death (Rev. 2:11);

and to those in Sardis:

He who overcomes shall be clothed in white garments, *and I will not blot out his name from the Book of Life*; but I will confess his name before My Father and before His angels (Rev. 3:5; emphasis added).

But both statements can be held to employ a figure of speech called "litotes," which is extremely common in literature and in everyday speech. Litotes is a way of making a positive affirmation by negating its opposite. The presence of litotes is often signaled by obvious understatement.

Thus when the author of Hebrews writes, "For God is not unjust to forget your work and labor of love . . . " (Heb. 6:10), it must be assumed that the reader already *knows* that God is never unjust or forgetful. The reader therefore correctly infers that the writer means something like: "God will keep your labor of love in mind and will stand by you accordingly."

Since a reader of the letter to Smyrna could be presumed to understand that no believer experiences the second death, the statement immediately suggests litotes. Jesus promises that the overcomer will certainly suffer no hurt from the second death. But this sharply understates what must be the destiny of the victorious Christian. Hence the reader is left with a tantalizing

inference like: "The experience of the overcomer is radically free
from the second death."

This inference is very natural in the light of the immediately
preceding words:

> Be faithful until death, and I will give you the crown of life
> (Rev. 2:10).

This can mean: "Die for Me, if need be, and you will enjoy the
crowning experience of life." Hence, in the promise to the overcomer, Jesus is saying something like this: "Though physical
death may touch you here, the second death cannot touch you
hereafter. Your experience will be much too wonderful for
that!"[7]

In a similar fashion, the words, "I will not blot out his name
from the Book of Life," at once suggest the understatement of a
litotes. No Christian will have his name blotted from that book.
His eternal identity rests on the fact that he is an individual
whose name is written in heaven (Luke 10:20). And that is just
the point. The litotes, taken in the light of the surrounding
statements, implies: "Your everlasting name is *supremely secure*.
For, as you stand clothed in a victor's garments, I will acknowledge that name in the august presence of My Father and before
the holy angels."[8]

Abundant and triumphant life, superlative and everlasting
honor, are thus the rewards held out to the struggling Christians
at Smyrna and Sardis. The use of litotes in both of these promises
is a way of imparting, through understatement, the delicate
suggestion that the experience will excel the description that is
given of it. Just as when someone says, "If you do this, you won't
regret it," he means, "Your recompense will be anything but
regret," so our Lord is saying to the overcomer that his reward
will be *anything but* injury from the second death or loss of an
eternal name!

But rewards they most assuredly are, as are all of the risen
Savior's promises to overcomers. And thus there is a sense in
which this final book of the biblical canon, through these challenging calls to victory, effectively punctuates the teaching of

the entire New Testament on the subject of spiritual conflict and eternal rewards.[9] The figure who emerges from these portraits is a conqueror, just as Jesus was Conqueror. The rewarded one is a victor worthy of co-heirship with the greatest Victor in human history.

And this is precisely the principle which is emphasized in the seventh and final promise to the overcomers:

> To him who overcomes I will grant to sit with Me on My
> throne, as I also overcame and sat down with My Father
> on His throne. He who has an ear, let him hear what the
> Spirit says to the churches (Rev. 3:21-22).

Such then is the call to joint-heirship. Such is the challenge of New Testament living. Its essence is superbly captured by a great hymn of the faith which needs to be sung in our day with increased appreciation:

> Am I a soldier of the cross,
> A follower of the Lamb?
> And shall I fear to own his cause,
> Or blush to speak His name?
>
> Must I be carried to the skies,
> On flowery beds of ease,
> While others fought to win the prize,
> And sailed through bloody seas.
>
> Since I must fight if I would reign,
> Increase my courage, Lord!
> I'll bear the toil, endure the pain,
> Supported by Thy Word.
>
> In the name of Christ the King,
> Who has purchased life for me,
> Thro' grace I'll win the promised crown,
> Whate'er my cross may be.[10]

The message in these words is biblical to the core. Accordingly, it simply remains that "he who has an ear" should "hear what the Spirit says to the churches"!

EPILOGUE

Even though Frank had dampened his spirits a bit, Jim continued to go to the group Bible study to learn all he could about rewards.

As an increasing number of passages in the New Testament were opened up to him, Jim saw the challenge of Christian living more clearly. He understood more deeply what the Bible meant when it said, "If we endure, we shall also reign with Him."

"I think I'll try to help Frank understand these things a little better," Jim said to himself. "I think he'll be thrilled when he realizes what it means to be an overcomer."

So the next day at work, on their break, the two Christian friends talked further about the meaning of Christian victory. It was the first of many such chats in the months that followed.

These were good days for Jim. He knew, of course, that struggles and trials lay along the path he had chosen. He was determined to trust God whenever these came. But the road was bright as he looked ahead—because it ended on a throne.

That was a healthy perspective to have. And if Jim could keep his heart focused on that, the shadows cast by the eclipse of grace would not darken his pathway anymore.

Notes

(After the first reference to an author's work, later references to the same work use a shortened form and the reader is referred back to the initial reference for full bibliographic details.)

Chapter 1

[1] For helpful discussions in this area, see Robert D. Preus, "Perennial Problems in the Doctrine of Justification," *Concordia Theological Quarterly* 45 (1981):163-184; and A.N.S. Lane, "Calvin's Doctrine of Assurance," *Vox Evangelica* 11 (1979): 32-54.

[2] For highly critical reviews of the statement (issued Sept. 30, 1983, by the Lutheran-Roman Catholic Dialogue Group) see W. Robert Godfrey, "Reversing the Reformation," *Eternity* 35 (Sept. 1984):26-28; and C.M. Gullerod, "U.S. Lutheran-Roman Catholic Dialogue on Justification by Faith: An Examination," *Journal of Theology* 24 (1984):19-24. For the statement itself consult, *Justification by Faith: Lutherans and Catholics in Dialogue,* 7 (to be published Spring/Summer, 1985, by the U.S.A. National Committee of the Lutheran World Federation and the Bishops' Committee for Ecumenical and Interreligious Affairs).

[3] For a recent example, see Samuel T. Logan, Jr., "The Doctrine of Justification in the Theology of Jonathan Edwards," *Westminster Theological Journal* 46 (1984):26-52. Note especially pp. 42-48. At least the approach represented here is candid in its admission that "evangelical obedience is an absolute necessity, a 'condition' in man's justification" (p. 43). But nothing can conceal that this is, in principle, a return to the Roman Catholic view that both faith and works are essential to final salvation. Though Logan would no doubt reject the charge, the position he maintains (following Edwards) reduces the great soteriological issues of the Protestant Reformation to little more than a problem in theological articulation. From the much superior perspective of John Calvin, Logan's view might be described as a *"de facto* justification by works"* (see the article by Lane in note 1, especially pp. 35 and 40). The same could be said of the view advanced by Daniel P. Fuller in *Gospel and Law: Contrast or Continuum?* (Grand Rapids: Eerdmans, 1980), pp. 65-120. Very serious questions have been raised recently concerning the extent to which Calvinism has departed from Calvin's own doctrine of faith and assurance. In addition to the article by Lane, see R.T. Kendall, *Calvin and English Calvinism to 1649* (Oxford: University Press, 1979).

[4] Note the harsh judgment of John H. Gerstner in *A Primer on Dispensationalism* (Phillipsburg, N.J.: Presbyterian and Reformed Publishing Co., 1982), p. 29.

[5] The primary New Testament words for repentance (verb, *metanoeō*; noun, *metanoia*) signify simply a change of mind. They *do not have* the sense of the English word for repentance which almost always suggests turning from sin, with overtones of sorrow and contrition. Every act of saving faith necessarily involves some change of mind since one cannot move from unbelief to faith without altering one's perspective. In that sense "repentance" is always involved in trusting Christ. But the notion that one must decide to abandon his sin in order to be saved is actually based on reading the English meaning of "repentance" into some New Testament texts. For valuable discussions of this subject, see Richard A. Seymour, *All About Repentance* (Hollywood, FL: Harvest House Publishers, 1974); and Robert Nicholas Wilkin, *Repentance as a Condition for Salvation in the New Testament* (unpublished Th.D. dissertation, Dallas Theological Seminary, 1985).

[6] See Moisés Silva, *Biblical Words and Their Meanings* (Grand Rapids: Zondervan, 1983), pp. 25-26; but especially, James Barr, *The Semantics of Biblical Language* (Oxford: University Press, 1961), pp. 217-219. Barr called this kind of error "illegitimate identity transfer."

[7]See *Theological Dictionary of the New Testament*, ed. by Gerhard Fried-rich, trans. and ed. by Geoffrey W. Bromiley (Grand Rapids: Eerdmans, 1968), 6:203.

[8]By far the most important recent discussion of saving faith (which this writer has seen) is the little volume by Gordon H. Clark entitled, *Faith and Saving Faith* (Jefferson, Md.: The Trinity Foundation, 1983). Clark vigorously rejects the many confused, and confusing, definitions of saving faith which are current today. See also note 2, chapter 2.

Chapter 2

[1]See F.F. Bruce, *The Epistle to the Galatians* (Grand Rapids: Eerdmans, 1982), p. 112.

[2]Faith has often been analyzed by theologians into *notitia* (understanding), *assensus* (assent), and *fiducia* (trust). Gordon Clark has rightly pointed out that the last of these (*fiducia*) involves a tautology, since it is like saying that faith includes faith. Clark's definitions of faith in general, and saving faith in partic-ular, are noteworthy: "Faith, by definition, is assent to understood propositions. Not all cases of assent, even assent to Biblical propositions, are saving faith; but all saving faith is assent to one or more Biblical propositions." It only needs to be added that, for John, the saving proposition to be believed is the one stated in John 20:30-31. Cf. *Faith and Saving Faith*, pp. 52 and 118 (see note 8, chapter 1). It may be pointed out also that trust in a person is no different than belief in some proposition about that person: for example, "Mr. Jones can be relied upon for this." Cf. Clark, pp. 106-107.

[3]Preus rightly rejects the opinion that justifying faith can be considered a good work (a Roman Catholic perspective shared by many Protestants). Instead, he affirms the Lutheran view "that faith's role in justification is purely instrumental, that faith is an *organum leptikon*, like the empty hand of a beggar receiving a gift, that it alone (*sola fide*) is the appropriate vehicle to receive reconciliation, forgiveness, Christ and His merits . . . ." Robert D. Preus, "Perennial Problems," p. 172 (see note 1, chapter 1).

[4]It has been suggested that "against the context of vss. 22ff," the phrase "*Go in by the narrow gate* will be understood as meaning that entrance into the Kingdom . . . is through a narrow gate." W.F. Albright and C.S. Mann, *Matthew*, Anchor Bible (New York: Doubleday, 1971), pp. 84-85.

[5]It is essentially correct to say with Beare that, "The Gospel according to Matthew may be described as a manual of instruction in the Christian way of life, which the author sees as the fulfillment in Jesus Christ of the revelation of God given to Israel and preserved in the sacred scriptures." Francis Wright Beare, *The Gospel according to Matthew* (Oxford: Basil Blackwell, 1981), p. 5. It does not follow, however, as Beare thinks, that "the promises made to Israel are now inherited by the church of Christ's foundation" or that Matthew teaches salvation by means of works-righteousness (p. 6). But it is a useful conception to describe this Gospel as a "manual of instruction in the Christian way of life."

Chapter 3

[1]It has been suggested that the thought of an imputed divine righteousness may be anticipated in Matthew by the Suffering Servant's own dedication to "fulfill all righteousness" (Matt. 3:15). See S. Craig Glickman, *The Temptation Account in Matthew and Luke* (unpublished Th.D. dissertation, University of Basel, 1982), pp. 37-44; esp., pp. 42-44. The Old Testament background for this idea is most clearly seen in Isaiah 53:10-12.

²It is correct to observe that some commentators on the Sermon on the Mount "tend to forget that the Great Instruction in Matthew was directed to the inner circle of the disciples, and not to the whole people." Albright and Mann, *Matthew*, p. 49 (see note 4, chapter 2). It is also true to say: "Nor is this salvation by Law or by works, as puzzled commentators on Matthew have been known to suggest" (pp. 51-52).

Chapter 4

¹For examples, see the Septuagint rendering of the following texts (English references are given here): Genesis 19:17; 32:30; 1 Samuel 19:11; Job 33:28; Psalm 31:7; 72:13; 109:31; Jeremiah 48:6; etc.

²The flexibility of the Greek word *psuche* is evident in Luke 12:19-20. In verse 19, it refers to the personal self whom the rich man addresses reflexively. In verse 20, it refers to the life he is about to lose. The paronomasia (word play) would appeal to the Greek ear, but it must be sacrificed in a fully accurate translation.

³For a succinct statement of the interpretation of "saving the life," as given in this chapter, see R.E. Neighbour, *If They Shall Fall Away* (reprint edition, Miami Springs, Fl.: Conley & Schoettle, 1984), pp. 29-30.

Chapter 5

¹For a discussion of the rabbinic perspective, see William E. Brown, *The New Testament Concept of the Believer's Inheritance* (unpublished Th.D. dissertation, Dallas Theological Seminary, 1984), pp. 34-40.

²Very appropriately it has been said, "in the greatly misunderstood incident of the rich young ruler, it is striking that every commandment quoted by our Lord is from the Second Table of the Law; not because in the observance of these social laws men could earn eternal life, but in order that the young man might be tested by his own claims of moral perfection and come to see himself as a sinner whose only hope is in what God can do (Matt. 19:19-26)." Alva J. McClain, *The Greatness of the Kingdom* (Grand Rapids: Zondervan, 1959)." p. 290. Ray Summers also observes that, "In his response, Jesus led the young ruler to see that not even a sincere effort at obedience to the law could give life. All the law could do was point him to his need and reflect his inability to keep it. The young man's downfall was in relation to the tenth command, 'You shall not covet.' " Ray Summers, *Commentary on Luke* (Waco, Tx.: Word Books, 1972), p. 214.

³The phrase "from my youth" may be a reference to his twelfth year, at which time Jewish youths assumed responsibility for obedience to the law's commands. See William L. Lane, *The Gospel According to Mark* (Grand Rapids: Eerdmans, 1974), p. 366. Lane cites the Mishnah (*Berachoth* II. 2) and Luke 2.42.

⁴Summers, *Luke*, p. 215 (see note 2, this chapter), thinks that the one thing which the young man lacked was love. This, too, would emphasize his failure and sinfulness. But since the young man's need for eternal life could not be met by any conceivable expression of love, it is more likely that our Lord is pointing to his most basic deficiency—faith.

⁵Naturally, some have tried to put Jesus' interview with the rich young man into the service of a doctrine of Lordship salvation. This is explicitly done by Walter J. Chantry, *Today's Gospel: Authentic or Synthetic?* (Edinburgh: Banner of Truth Trust, 1970). For an effective critique of Lordship teaching, see G. Michael Cocoris, *Lordship Salvation—Is It Biblical?* (Dallas: Redención Viva, 1983).

[6]Lane is not correct to observe that, "The assurance of 'treasure in heaven' reflects an idiom that was current in Judaism, which allowed Jesus to enter the thought-world of his contemporaries. Here, however, it is stripped of its customary associations of merit (as if selling one's property and giving the money received to the poor will *earn* a significant reward), since the promised treasure signifies the gift of eternal life or salvation at the revelation of the Kingdom of God." Lane, *Mark*, p. 367 (see note 3, this chapter). It is entirely gratuitous to read into Jesus' words the concept of "the gift of eternal life." Rather, our Lord stands fully within the contemporary Jewish "thought-world" in associating "treasure in heaven" with meritorious behavior.

[7]The statement quoted from Mark 10:24 is not found in two famous ancient manuscripts: the Codex Vaticanus (B) and Codex Sinaiticus (Aleph). A few other witnesses also support the omission. But the longer text is overwhelmingly attested in the vast majority of the surviving Greek manuscripts of Mark. The accidental omission of a "colon" (sense-line) in a common ancestor of Aleph and B is perhaps the source of the omission. The adoption of the omission as the original reading by many modern editors and translators reflects an inappropriately high regard for the two manuscripts in question. But even so, the truth affirmed by Mark 10:24 is self-evident when the story is reflected on properly.

[8]"Jesus believed that heaven will be richer for one who has used earthly riches in good stewardship to God and compassion for needy men." Summers, *Luke*, p. 215 (see note 2, this chapter).

Chapter 6

[1]This truth is very effectively presented by Alexander Patterson, *The Greater Life and Work of Christ* (New York: Fleming H. Revell, 1896), pp. 314-316.

[2]On this theme, G. Campbell Morgan writes: "'We must all be made manifest'; for God does not dissociate our work from ourselves. Outward efforts count for nothing unless I am a Christ-soul; and then my life is my work. The question of each one should be, Of what sort is my life? If it is self-centered and unwatchful, so also is my work—'wood, hay, stubble' (1 Cor. iii. 12). But if my life is surrendered to the King, if I am loyal to Him and absolutely under His control, mine is King's work—'gold, silver, precious stones.'" G. Campbell Morgan, *God's Methods With Man* (New York: Fleming H. Revell, 1898), pp. 90-91.

[3]On this text, see the helpful little article by John A. Sproul, " 'Judgment Seat' or 'Awards Podium,'" *Spire* (published by Grace Theological Seminary, Winona Lake, Ind.) 13 (1984):3-5.

[4]It is worth mentioning that in Romans 2:4-10 Paul refers to the principle we are discussing, namely, that God will repay men according to their works. The Apostle's perspective is distinctly eschatological. The wrath to which he refers (Rom. 2:5, 8-9) is undoubtedly the wrath which will be poured out during the Great Tribulation. Moreover, eternal life is presented as a reward for "patient continuance in doing good" (v. 7). Here we meet again the principle we encountered in connection with the rich young ruler. Eternal life, viewed as an eschatological attainment, is indeed a reward for doing good. But Paul knows well that it is also a gift (Rom. 6:23) and that no man is ever justified by doing good (Rom. 4:4-5). No one can thus obtain eternal life as a reward who does not first find justification and life as a free gift (Rom. 5:18; see vv. 12-21). Paul's argument in Romans 2 is directed at the self-righteous sinner who, despite his self-righteousness, is guilty before God (Rom 2:1). Such a man needs to know that, in the eschatological era that is coming, men will get only what they deserve from God (2:2-11). This principle is affirmed by Paul as a means of driving the self-righteous person to sense his need of justifying grace. Romans

2:13 has the same force: if one expects justification by the law, one must keep the law. But no one does, as Paul will later insist (Rom. 3:19). It is unfortunate that Romans 2:7, 10, and 13 have sometimes been taken in such a way as to contradict fundamental Pauline doctrine. There is no need for this to be done.

Chapter 7

[1]The opinion is now widely held that Luke-Acts was written with a Christian audience in view. See, for example, Robert Maddox, *The Purpose of Luke— Acts* (Edinburgh: T & T Clark, 1982). If the author is seen as Luke, the companion of Paul, the Christian community to which Theophilus belonged is likely to have had connections with Paul.

[2]Mark Antony was Herod's patron, and it was the Roman Senate that conferred on Herod the title of king. He was also equipped with an army which he used to conquer Judea. One can scarcely miss the analogy with Christ, who will return to earth with a heavenly army and conquer His enemies (Rev. 19:11-21). The informed Christian reader of Luke's parable would have no trouble in seeing the comparison which is implied.

Chapter 8

[1]Although it is very common to equate "entering" the Kingdom with "inheriting" it, this equation is not universally made. See the extended discussion of the difference in Kenneth F. Dodson, *The Prize of the Up-Calling* (Grand Rapids: Baker Book House, 1969), pp. 121-142. In the Septuagint the expression "to inherit a/the kingdom" apparently does not occur. The closest analogy to this seems to be 1 Maccabees 2:57, "David, because he was merciful, inherited the throne of the kingdom for ever." See *The Oxford Annotated Apocrypha*, ed. by Bruce M. Metzger (New York: Oxford University Press, 1977), p. 226. But it should be pointed out that the very similar idea, "to inherit the land," is frequent in the sense of "to possess (own) the land." Moreover, the difference between "entering" and "inheriting" the land can be seen in 1 Esdras 8:83 ("'The land which you are entering to take possession of [Greek, inherit] it is a land polluted . . . .'" And in Nehemiah 9:15 ("And told them to go in to possess [Greek, inherit] the land . . . ."). In these texts the action of "entering" the land is antecedent to, and for the purpose of, "taking possession" of the land. The actions involved are *not* synonymous.

[2]For a good summary of the rights and role of the firstborn son in Old Testament thought, see Erich Sauer, *In the Arena of Faith* (London: Paternoster Press, 1955), pp. 127-131. For the view that firstborn rights may be forfeited by unfaithful Christians (who are nevertheless eternally saved), see G.H. Lang, *Firstborn Sons: Their Rights and Risks*, 2nd ed. (London: Oliphants, 1943). Lang thought, however, that failing Christians would be excluded from the millennial Kingdom. See also note 3, chapter 9.

[3]Romans 8:17 distinguishes the two kinds of heirship as clearly as any text. The concept of joint-heirship is communicated by Paul through a sequence of words using the Greek prefix *sun-*, which is roughly equivalent to our prefix co-. We may paraphrase the text for purposes of clarity as follows: "And if we are children, we are also heirs—on the one hand heirs of God, and on the other hand co-heirs with Christ, providing that we co-suffer that we may also be co-glorified." The distinction is nicely picked up by Dodson, *Prize*, pp. 134-135 (see note 1, this chapter).

[4]The Greek word *meros* (Rev. 20:6; Lk. 15:12) is used once in the Septuagint (Prov. 17:2) to translate the Hebrew word *naḥal* (inheritance, possession). The word *meris* is the one usually used in the Greek Old Testament to render *heleq*

(portion), although *meros* stands for *heleq* once (Eccl. 5:18). *Meris* is rare in the New Testament (5 times, all in Luke and Paul), while *meros* is common (about 40 times). It is highly probable that for New Testament writers other than Luke and Paul *meros* has largely replaced *meris* in the sense of "portion" (= inheritance).

[5]Totally misconceived is the statement of Margaret Pamment that, "The Beatitudes offer encouragement and consolation, and they indicate the characteristics of those who will enter the kingdom, and thereby the conditions of entry." Margaret Pamment, "The Kingdom of Heaven According to the First Gospel," *New Testament Studies* 27 (1981):213. The premise of this statement is wrong and so is the conclusion. Matthew in no way indicates that such character traits are conditions for *entering* the Kingdom. But, clearly, the Kingdom *belongs* to those with such qualifications: Matthew 5:3 and 10 "frame" the Beatitudes. Verses 11-12 speak in terms of *reward*.

[6]See the treatment of Esau by Erich Sauer, *Arena*, pp. 126-127; 152-153; 161-162 (see note 8, this chapter).

[7]One should compare the warning of Paul against similar conduct in 1 Thessalonians 5:4-8.

[8]A very similar parable is found in Luke 12:42-46. It is followed, in verses 47-48, by a reference to the flogging of disobedient servants. Those who were ignorantly disobedient receive fewer lashes of the whip than those who disobeyed while knowing their Master's will. Here, too, we should conclude that metaphor is at work. The lashes then can refer to the stinging rebukes which the Lord will give to unfaithful servants. No doubt these will be deeply felt by those servants precisely because they are now holy and fully sensitive to their Master's feelings about them.

[9]In the similar parable of Luke 12:42-46, instead of the designation "the hypocrites," we find the Greek words *tōn apistōn*. These words should be rendered "the unfaithful," as the context shows, rather than as "the unbelievers" (NKJV).

[10]The phrase in Luke 19:12, 15 uses the Greek verb *lambanō* whereas the Septuagint expression used the synonym *paralambanō*. For references, see note 11 following.

[11]As is well known, the author of Hebrews is steeped in the Greek Old Testament. Here he uses a Septuagintal phrase (*paralambanein basileian*) which meant "to obtain the power of kingship." See the Septuagint rendering of the following passages (references are to the English text): Daniel 5:31, 6:28; 7:18; Bel and the Dragon (Apocrypha) 1; 2 Maccabees (Apocrypha) 4:7; 10:11. The original readers of Hebrews knew precisely what the author meant. One might even suspect an allusion to Daniel 7:18.

Chapter 9

[1]A recent commentator has said, "With respect to form, Ps 45 is basically a *royal psalm*; specifically, it is described in the title (v 1) as a *love song*, and the substance indicates that the love song should be interpreted as a *wedding song* . . . . There are no precise parallels to this type of psalm elsewhere in the Psalter . . . ." (Emphasis in the original.) Peter C. Craigie, *Psalms 1-50*, Word Biblical Commentary (Waco, TX: Word Books, 1983), p. 337. No doubt the great beauty and uniqueness of the psalm both contributed to its influence on New Testament thought.

[2]See Joachim Jeremias, *The Parables of Jesus*, revised ed. (New York: Charles Scribner's Sons, 1963), p. 65.

[3]It is right for G.H. Lang to say of the "outer darkness" that, "Few expressions have been treated with more laxity and liberty than this, though, seeing its

solemnity, it should have received very exact study." G.H. Lang, *The Parabolic Teaching of Scripture* (Grand Rapids: Eerdmans, 1956), p. 305. His point is well taken and his general discussion of the term is outstanding (pp. 305-308). Most of the observations made by the present writer are anticipated by Lang. See also, "The Outer Darkness," *The Star of Hope* (published by the Southern Hebrew Mission, Inc.) 7 (August-September, 1964):1-4 (but the accuracy of some of the references found in this article is open to question). It needs to be pointed out that many of those who have not taken the "outer darkness" as a description of eternal damnation have thought that the failing servant of Christ was to be excluded from the millennial Kingdom. But this involves a misperception of the imagery employed and contradicts the promise of 1 Thessalonians 5:9-10 which guarantees to the watchful and unwatchful the privilege of living together with Christ. See Zane C. Hodges, "The Rapture in 1 Thessalonians 5:1-11," in *Walvoord: A Tribute*, ed. by Donald K. Campbell (Chicago: Moody Press, 1982), pp. 67-79.

[4]Thayer correctly observes: "the darkness outside the limits of the lighted palace . . . ." Joseph Henry Thayer, *A Greek-English Lexicon of the New Testament* (New York: American Book Company, 1889), p. 226.

[5]One should remember, in connection with "weeping and gnashing of teeth," that the Oriental is very demonstrative in the expression of grief. The phrase only sounds extreme to reserved Westerners. See G.H. Lang, *Parabolic Teaching*, p. 306 (see note 3, this chapter).

[6]See G.H. Lang, *Parabolic Teaching*, p. 306 (see note 3, this chapter).

[7]Sauer summarizes these truths well: "Justification is a gift of free grace, but the measure of glorification depends upon personal devotion and steadfastness in the race." Erich Sauer, *Arena*, p. 162 (see not 8, chapter 8). See Sauer's whole discussion, pp. 161-166.

Chapter 10

[1]Compare the hymn, "When He Shall Come," by Almeda J. Pearce.

[2]Bruce artfully interprets: "Ye have done nobly, and noble shall be your reward . . . ." Alexander Balmain Bruce, *The Parabolic Teaching of Christ* (New York: A.C. Armstrong & Son, 1892), p. 493.

[3]It may be pointed out that Matthew 24:13, or its parallel in 10:22, played a role in Augustinian theology. (See *On the Gift of Perseverance*, chapter 2.) According to Augustine, perseverance to the end is a divine gift necessary for final salvation. He states that "it is uncertain whether anyone has received this gift so long as he is still alive" (chapter 1). Thus, for Augustine, there could be no assurance of one's election before death. Indeed, all who insist on perseverance to the end as a sign of genuine faith must likewise abandon the doctrine of assurance. Augustine, however, held that one could possess true faith and lose it (chapter 1). So in his view a man could be a true Christian for a time, yet not elect!

[4]Ladd holds that the "brethren" of this parable are Jesus' disciples who preach the good news about the Kingdom of God. This is similar to, but obviously not identical with, the view taken by the present writer. See George Eldon Ladd, "The Parable of the Sheep and the Goats in Recent Interpretation," in *New Dimensions in New Testament Study* (Grand Rapids: Zondervan, 1974), 197-199. Ladd, of course, does not hold to a pre-tribulation rapture of the Church. Of course, young children below the age of accountability are not in view in Matthew 25. Perhaps they will grow up in, and repopulate, the Kingdom (see Matt. 19:14).

[5]Compare in the Greek Old Testament the references to "giving" someone a kingdom: for example, 2 Samuel 16:8; 2 Chronicles 21:3; Daniel 2:37; 7:27. The references are to the English text.

[6]J. William Fuller, "'I Will Not Erase His Name from the Book of Life' (Revelation 3:5)," *Journal of the Evangelical Theological Society* 26 (1983):299. He goes on to say, "Surely the burden of proof is on the shoulders of those who would argue that the warnings are not genuinely addressed to true believers as they seem to be and that the promises are genuinely addressed to all believers (as they seem not to be). Hence the 'overcomer' is the individual Christian who enjoys special benefits in eternity for refusing to give up his faith in spite of persecution during life on earth" (p. 299). Of course, this general view of the "overcomers" of Revelation 2 and 3 has a long and respectable exegetical history. See, for example. J.N. Darby, *Synopsis of the Books of the Bible*, 5: *Colossians—The Revelation* (Kingston-On-Thames: Stow Hill Bible and Tract Depot, 1949 printing):380; William Kelly, *Lectures on the Book of Revelation*, new ed. (London: G. Morrish, n.d.), p. 36; Walter Scott, *Exposition of the Revelation of Jesus Christ*, 4th ed. (London: Pickering & Inglis, n.d.), pp. 64-65

[7]Tatford clearly thinks in terms of litotes when he writes of the promise of Revelation 2:11, "True life lay beyond. In no wise should he be touched by the second death and the very form of the expression but emphasizes the certainty of that truer and fuller life." Fredk. A. Tatford, *Prophecy's Last Word* (London: Pickering & Inglis, 1947), p. 46.

[8]Tatford again interprets through litotes when he writes of Revelation 3:5, "Practically every city of that day kept a role or register of its citizens . . . . one who had performed some great exploit deserving of special distinction, was honoured by having his name inscribed in golden letters in the citizens' roll. Our Lord's emphatic statement, therefore, implies not merely that the name of the overcomer shall not be expunged, but *per contra* that it shall be inscribed in golden letters in the heavenly roll." His whole discussion here is worth reading. Fredk. A. Tatford, *Prophecy's Last Word*, p. 63; see pp. 62-63 (see previous note).

[9]Alexander Patterson weaves together many strands of truth when he writes about the Judgment Seat of Christ, "Not a service done for Christ loses its reward. 'For his sake,' is the criterion by which everything is to be judged. The sacrifices of the believer are then shown and rewarded. It is then the Beatitudes are completely fulfilled. Then those who have laid up treasure in heaven receive it with manifold interest. All losses are made good. Then it is the promises are fulfilled, made 'to him that overcometh.' It is then the righteous 'shine forth as the sun in the kingdom of their Father.' At this time the faithful servants are rewarded for good use of their pounds and talents . . . . The rewards are of glory, power, and privilege. The glory, as has been shown by Paul, differs as one star differs from another. The power, as the ruler over ten cities is superior to the ruler over one city. Among the privileges seems to be nearness to the person of Christ. There were two who asked that they might sit on his right hand and left. Christ said this was to be given to those for whom it was prepared. . . . In the distribution of rewards it is not against one that he came in at the eleventh hour." Alexander Patterson, *The Greater Life and Work of Christ*, p. 316 (see note 1, chapter 6). This beautiful résumé of rewards truth was written in the nineteenth century. How little of it is understood in the twentieth!

[10]"A Soldier of the Cross," by Isaac Watts.